D-DAY WEST SUSSEX

Springboard for the Normandy Landings
1944

Ian Greig

Kim Leslie

Alan Readman

west sussex county council

First published in 1994 by

West Sussex County Council

County Hall

Chichester

West Sussex

PO19 1RQ

Telephone: 0243 777100

Fax: 0243 777952

ISBN 0 86260 291 2

Cover

Photograph of tank movement between Petworth
and Waterlooville en route to Normandy by
*courtesy of the **Imperial War Museum***

D-Day 50th Anniversary Year logo by courtesy of

Southern Tourist Board

40 Chamberlayne Road

Eastleigh

Hampshire

SO5 5JH

Telephone: *0703 620006*

Fax: *0703 620010*

Design by   *Morwenna Wells*

Typeset by   *WSCC Word Processing Centre*

Printed by   *Selsey Press*

                        84 High Street

                        Selsey

                        West Sussex

                        PO20 0QH

CONTENTS

... the southern portion of England became one vast camp, dump and airfield ... Passenger traffic practically ceased and even essential commodities were transported with difficulty. Construction of the great artificial harbours engaged the services of thousands of men and added indescribable congestion to already crowded ports and harbours ... Sustained by the certainty that a decisive effort was in the offing and inspired by the example and leadership of Winston Churchill, people cheerfully accepted the need of using their own streets and roads at the risk of being run down, of seeing their fields and gardens trampled, of waiting in long queues for trains that rarely arrived, and of suffering a further cut in an already meagre ration so that nothing should interfere with the movement of the soldiers and the mountains of supplies we so lavishly consumed.

General Dwight D. Eisenhower
Crusade in Europe
(Heinemann, 1948, p. 262)

Preface
by
Dame Vera Lynn DBE

I am very happy to be invited to write a preface to the story of D-Day and West Sussex. Recalling the months leading up to 6 June 1944 will bring back memories for thousands of soldiers, sailors and airmen who came to live and train in the county for their own special part in the Normandy landings.

This is the first time that the contribution of West Sussex to the D-Day preparations has been told in such detail. It weaves together the experiences of the armed forces with the memories of local people on the home front. West Sussex played a crucial part in the invasion planning when so much of our future and security was at stake.

I can well remember these difficult times when the outcome was so uncertain, when we owed such a lot to those who fought so bravely in this great military crusade fifty years ago. D-Day was a turning point in the war and I am delighted to be associated with this record of what was achieved in West Sussex to help ensure our ultimate victory.

Vera Lynn

All southern England was one vast military camp, crowded with soldiers awaiting final word to go, and piled high with supplies and equipment awaiting transport to the far shore of the Channel. The whole area was cut off from the rest of England. The government had established a deadline, across which no unauthorized person was allowed to go in either direction. Every separate encampment, barrack, vehicle park, and every unit was carefully charted on our master maps. The scheduled movement of each unit had been so worked out that it would reach the embarkation point at the exact time the vessels would be ready to receive it. The southernmost camps where assault troops were assembled were all surrounded by barbed-wire entanglements to prevent any soldier leaving the camp after he had once been briefed as to his part in the attack. The whole mighty host was tense as a coiled spring, and indeed that is exactly what it was - a great human spring, coiled for the moment when its energy should be released and it would vault the English Channel in the greatest amphibious assault ever attempted.

General Dwight D. Eisenhower
Crusade in Europe
(Heinemann, 1948, p. 273)

INTRODUCTION

This commemorative history seeks to outline the vital part played by West Sussex in the D-Day offensive of 1944 during World War Two.

Even after all these years, and countless books on the subject of D-Day, the West Sussex contribution to this momentous story has never been told before. Locally little documentary material exists at all, to a large extent a comment on the effectiveness of the veil of secrecy and censorship imposed during the wartime emergency.

This present publication is substantially based on original documents, hitherto unpublished, held in the Public Record Office at Kew.

To this nationally-held material have been added recollections of those who either lived or served in the county during the D-Day preparations. These are being collected together as an archive at the West Sussex Record Office as a result of an appeal in local newspapers in late 1993. As we go to press these reminiscences continue to come in and are adding a substantial amount of new - and unofficial - information, especially about how ordinary civilians reacted to what was going on around their homes as the military took over. We hope this book will bring in even more recollections for this permanent archive in the Record Office.

A great deal of gratitude is owed to many people in giving help and encouragement during the compilation of this book.

A substantial proportion of the research was conducted in the Public Record Office, and for this we are most grateful to the Keeper, Sarah Tyacke, and her staff.

For the use of information and facilities in the West Sussex Record Office we owe much to the new County Archivist, Richard Childs, for all his support and help in making this project possible.

The Imperial War Museum in London has been of immense help, and we are particularly indebted to the Keeper of the Department of Documents, Roderick Suddaby, and to the Keeper of the Department of Photographs, Jane Carmichael.

A great deal of advice, support and knowledge has been received from Ken Rimell, Co-Director of the Museum of D-Day Aviation, until recently at the site of the RAF Advanced Landing Ground at Apuldram, and now from 1994 at Shoreham Airport, whose infectious enthusiasm has been a constant source of encouragement.

Many others have helped by either providing information, or their own recollections, a good many of which are directly quoted in the text. Especial thanks are due to Barbara Bertram, Myra Bigg, Barbara Brimblecombe, Don Broughton, John Clery, Peter Cruden, Keith Downer, Peter Driscoll, Joan Edom, Clifford Fidler, Joan and Ron Ham, Maurice Henly, Leslie Howell, Ron Iden, Lois Jordan, Winifred Langer, Mary Lochner, Irene MacDonald, Robin McNish, Charles Messenger, Georgina Morrieson, Adrian Poole, Flora MacDonald Roberts, Clifford Robinson, Douglas Robinson, Pat Roth, Pat Saunders, Eric Skilton, Keith Smith, Joan Strange, Pamela Waldy, Derek Walker, Connie Westerdick, Jim Wheeler, Sally White, Paddy Whiteside, Rex Williams and Maurice Wilson-Voke.

The technical production of this book at County Hall - against a very tight schedule for its launch in

INTRODUCTION

April 1994 to mark General Eisenhower's stay in Chichester in April 1944 - has only been made possible by Morwenna Wells, our designer, and Anne Waite, Sally Anderson and Martin O'Neill of the County Secretariat, and David Nicholls of Selsey for his photography.

Finally may we dedicate this commemorative record to the memory of all those army, air and naval personnel and people of West Sussex who played their part in the build-up to D-Day fifty years ago.

Ian Greig
Kim Leslie
Alan Readman

CHAPTER I

THE CHALLENGE

'Okay, we'll go.'[1]

With these words spoken in the early hours of 5 June 1944 - after days of agonising deliberation over the weather - General Dwight D. Eisenhower, Commander of Supreme Headquarters Allied Expeditionary Force (SHAEF), set in motion the greatest armada the world has ever seen. It was an armada which was to employ 4,200 landing ships and landing craft, and over 1,200 merchant ships. The whole was to be protected by over 1,000 warships, and by immense air power, and to be supplemented by airborne forces carried in 1,078 transport planes and gliders.

SHAEF
The flaming sword of justice avenges the black of Nazi oppression. Above, the rainbow of hope symbolises the peace to come.

At the opening of a campaign which was to end the war in Europe in just under a year, nearly one million men were scheduled to be carried to the Normandy coast in the first three weeks after the assault forces stormed the landing beaches at H-Hour on D-Day. Before another three weeks were out the total involved was nearly two million troops, together with 365,000 vehicles.

Early in 1943, over a year before the armada was launched, Lieutenant-General Sir Frederick Morgan was designated as Chief of Staff to the Supreme Allied Commander (COSSAC) to lead the Anglo-American planning staff responsible for drawing up the main outline of Operation Overlord. This was the code-name for the planned allied landings in Normandy and subsequent advance into Germany. In his first report General Morgan cautioned that

> An operation of the magnitude of **Operation Overlord** has never previously been attempted in history. It is fraught with hazards, both in nature and magnitude, which do not obtain in any other theatre of the present world war. Unless these hazards are squarely faced and adequately overcome, the operation cannot succeed. There is no reason why they should not be overcome, provided the energies of all concerned are bent to the problem.[2]

The story of how these hazards were overcome, in what was without doubt one of the most complicated and brilliant pieces of strategic planning of all time, has filled many books. But even besides the mass of strategic, tactical and technical problems relating to the actual assault on the Normandy beaches, an additional problem of immense size confronted the allied planners. This was how to organise the huge

1 **Road Widening**
Road widening and bridge strengthening were major priorities to cope with invasion traffic to the South Coast. One month before D-Day a demolition gang breaks up one of Britain's front-line defences, a pillbox, to ease the flow of heavy vehicles and equipment. Its destruction marks the changing wartime strategy: from one of defence in the early part of the war - most pillboxes were built in 1940 when invasion was threatened - to the offensive position of 1944.

Operation Overlord

THE CHALLENGE

*2 **Thunderbolt Convoy***

All roads were cleared for heavy military convoys. RAF transporters carry American P-47 Thunderbolts to their new bases, March 1944. In the D-Day build-up Thunderbolts operated for short periods at Ford, Shoreham and Westhampnett.

concentration of men, fighting and transport vehicles and supplies required to ensure the assault would be a success.

In essence this involved the movement and concentration, within easy reach of embarkation ports, of some thirty-eight divisions each consisting of approximately 15,000 to 20,000 men equipped with a minimum of 3,000 vehicles. This had to be accomplished over a road system very short of today's standards and a railway network already stretched to the utmost by existing wartime demands. The whole operation needed to be completed within only four months in conditions of the greatest secrecy, the constant threat of enemy air attack and the possible use of enemy secret weapons whose full effects could not yet be foretold.

Of the manner in which the task was carried out, involving massive arrangements for feeding and care of the troops and the most intricate movement control, one military historian has written that

> Its accomplishment remains the greatest organizational achievement of the Second World War, a feat of staff - work that has dazzled history, a monument to the imagination and brilliance of thousands of British and American planners and logisticians which may never be surpassed in war. [3]

If the plan of the German High Command for the invasion of Britain in 1940 had ever been carried out, a major part of the assault would have fallen on the Sussex coast. Now, nearly four years later, Sussex was to become an important part of a crowded coastal springboard - stretching from Falmouth to Harwich - for an offensive which would take the allies to the heart of Germany.

All through the early weeks of 1944, then the spring and deep into the summer, army units of every size, type and role, including some of the most famous regiments in the British Army, poured down the county's roads into their camps and billets.

*3 **Armoured Invasion***

Troops, supplies and armoured vehicles poured into West Sussex before D-Day.

Situated between Newhaven - from which some 162,000 men sailed for France between D-Day and the end of July - and the chief embarkation ports in Hampshire, West Sussex was clearly destined for a major role as a Concentration Area for the forces gathering for Operation Overlord.

In March the headquarters of the British 21st Army Group, commanded by General Sir Bernard Montgomery, decided that the area between Newhaven and Portsmouth should be used for the concentration of units of both the 1st Corps, scheduled to assault Sword and Juno Beaches, and the 30th Corps scheduled to assault Gold Beach. By late May there were few places in West Sussex without at least one unit - often many more - awaiting the signal for D-Day.

CHAPTER 2

EARLY DAYS

Canadian Prelude

From the autumn of 1941 to early 1944 the defence of the Sussex coast was largely in the hands of the 1st Canadian Army. This was the largest force of British Commonwealth Dominion troops ever to be quartered in the United Kingdom at one time. Many units of the 1st, 2nd and 3rd Canadian Infantry Divisions and other formations spent many months in West Sussex. Together with British troops, they became involved in a series of large-scale and highly testing exercises across Southern England. As the months and years went by these exercises became less and less concerned with training for the defence of the United Kingdom against enemy invasion, but more and more with a cross-Channel offensive for the liberation of Europe.

In the summer of 1942 disaster overtook the 2nd Canadian Infantry Division, a formation then largely based in West Sussex. From camps at Fittleworth, Pulborough, Billingshurst, Petworth and Littlehampton, and many other towns and villages, units such as The Cameron Highlanders of Canada, The Royal Regiment of Canada, The Toronto Scottish, The Essex Scottish, The Fusiliers Mont-Royal, The South Saskatchewan Regiment, set out for Newhaven, Shoreham and the Solent ports on 18 August for what was by far the biggest cross-Channel raid of the war. They were to meet such murderous enemy fire on the beaches of Dieppe the next morning that many were mown down within a few yards of leaving the landing craft.

Disaster was further compounded by a garbled wireless message resulting in the premature abandoning of all efforts to evacuate a large body of survivors. This left no alternative but surrender and capture by the German defenders.

Out of a total raiding force of some 6,000 men - including some British Commandos - no fewer than 3,367 were killed, wounded or captured.

Some units were decimated. Only a few exhausted survivors reached the Royal Regiment's base at Littlehampton that night. Little more than a dozen men appeared on morning parade the next day. At nearby Middleton-on-Sea the morning muster of the Essex Scottish presented an almost equally pitiful spectacle: 'The sun is bright but the day is a sombre one' recorded the battalion war diary. [1]

The catastrophe of the ill-starred Dieppe raid has often been cited as having provided invaluable lessons which greatly contributed to the success of the D-Day landings. That some lessons were learnt seems certain. Some experts and military historians, however, have openly wondered if they might have been learnt without such heavy losses.

2nd British Army

Despite such casualties the 2nd Canadian Infantry Division was soon rebuilt. It went on to play a prominent part in the Normandy campaign and the subsequent fighting in North-West Europe until the end of the war. The 3rd Canadian Infantry Division became one of the 2nd British Army's three assault divisions on D-Day and was involved in several rehearsals for this role in Bracklesham Bay, near Chichester.

During the Canadian Army's stay in West Sussex a strong connection developed between the Canadian formations and the battalions of the county's Home Guard. The Canadians organised a

number of special training courses for the local Home Guard.

Today the Canadian-Sussex wartime connection is still perpetuated by visits of Canadian Army veteran associations to the county. Regular visits are paid by the veterans of the Toronto Scottish Regiment to Petworth where they were stationed. A special Dieppe raid memorial service is held each year in Wisborough Green as the headquarters of one of the 2nd Canadian Division brigades was nearby at Hawkhurst Court.

Desert Veterans in Worthing

One of the first indications of coming events in the county in the opening weeks of 1944 was instructions issued by Army Headquarters Sussex District for the billeting of the 4th Armoured Brigade in Worthing.

Royal Tank Regiment

The brigade consisted of The Royal Scots Greys, the 3rd County of London Yeomanry, the 44th Battalion The Royal Tank Regiment and the 2nd Battalion The King's Royal Rifle Corps. The 4th Armoured Brigade was one of the most battle-experienced formations in the British Army. It had taken a prominent part in all the major engagements of the 8th Army in the North African desert in the previous two years, including the battle of El Alamein and the pursuit of Rommel's Afrika Korps to Tunis. More recently it had taken a major part in the Italian campaign.

Still in action in Italy until the middle of December 1943, the brigade was now brought to Britain under conditions of the greatest secrecy in company with a considerable number of other ex-8th Army formations to take part in the forthcoming allied offensive.

The brigade's senior armoured regiment, the Scots Greys, sailed for home from Naples on

Rabbit Patrol

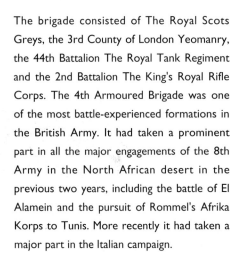

I drew back the curtains. There was an early morning mist but faintly I could make out strange shapes.

On the lawn were rows and rows of tents, and in the orchard beyond tanks were parked under the apple trees. In the Tudor rose garden a soldier was shaving, his mirror hanging from a rose bush.

The Canadians had arrived. Without warning they had come in the night, surrounding our old farmhouse at Lackenhurst, near Brooks Green, to the south-west of Horsham. There were tanks, lorries and jeeps. We had slept through it all and never heard a thing.

Father was in the army. When he came back on leave the way to his own front door was barred by sentries: 'No entry, you're not on our list.' 'But *I* live here!' barked back my father, 'and haven't slept for two nights and want a bath.' Three hours later he got into his own house.

It was a lovely sunny day and a Canadian officer was pushing me on my swing. Mother stood and watched. 'She reminds me of my little girl' he told her. 'I wonder if I'll ever see her again?'

Mother and I used to visit two elderly ladies who lived at Newbuildings, a big house nearby. She took them rabbit meat to eke out their meagre rations. She decided to walk through the woods as we always did even though it was now a military camp.

We took a short cut into the woods. The whole area had been transformed into an open air paint shop. Everywhere amphibious vehicles were being painted grey. The spray covered the trees, turning the whole wood an eerie grey. At the end of the camp we reached a check point guarded by two military policemen. Raising their rifles they challenged us: 'What's your business? What's in the basket?' 'Rabbits' said mother. 'Pull the other one, it's got bells on it' came back the unbelieving reply. She whisked back the cloth covering the top of the basket - side by side were snuggled the limp bodies of two freshly skinned rabbits! We were quickly waved on, his

white-gloved hand in our faces.

The next time we did the trip to the old ladies the same men were on duty. When they saw us coming, basket in hand again, one of them shouted 'OK, its only rabbit patrol.' They saluted, their faces lit up with big smiles. Shortly before the Canadians left we were warned about their testing their field gun. They hoped the blast wouldn't damage the old house and we should leave the windows unlatched. The next day we laid down on the floor with hands tightly over our ears. There was an enormous bang, all the windows rattled, but weren't broken.

Three weeks later the garden wall fell down!

All civilians had been told to keep off the road if a convoy approached. They moved quite fast and couldn't stop in a hurry so it would be easy to be run over.

Mother and I were cycling to Coolham to collect our rations from the village stores when we heard a rumble in the distance. A convoy was coming. We got off our bicycles and looked around for somewhere to go, but there was only a narrow verge and then a deep ditch and hedge. As the first tank was nearly upon us we threw ourselves, bicycles and all, into the ditch. An endless stream of vehicles passed by. The noise was deafening. At last the convoy passed and we both crawled from the ditch covered in dust.

We learnt later that the convoy was on its way to the coast. The invasion of France had begun.

Georgina Morrieson [2]

28 January 1944. The last time it had been stationed at home had been in the summer of 1938. Since then it had seen almost continuous active service. First engaged in helping to quell the Arab revolt in Palestine, it had subsequently taken part in the Syrian campaign. Exchanging its famous grey mounts for tanks it had then seen fighting in all the major desert battles since 1942. In Italy its tanks had been amongst the first ashore in the bitterly fought Salerno landings.

Any idea that the regiment was being brought home for a rest was quickly dispelled when it landed at Rothesay in Scotland, ten days after leaving Naples. The acting brigade commander at once informed the colonel of the regiment that it was booked to play a prominent role in the allied offensive against Hitler's Fortress Europe. They reached Worthing soon after midnight on 10 February, settling into billets in the Steyne and adjacent houses. The 4th Armoured Brigade headquarters was set up in Eardley House Hotel on Marine Parade, and other units moved into various parts of the town.

4 **Warnes Hotel, Worthing**
HQ for Royal Army Medical Corps and Royal Army Service Corps units in the build-up to D-Day.

Operation
Overlord

EARLY DAYS

Wartime Worthing

For almost a year now it had been difficult to come to the South Coast. We were constantly being stopped by the police for identity cards to ensure we had the right to be in Worthing at all.

Roads and lanes for miles around were packed with military stores of all kinds: ammunition dumps, vehicle parks and huge troop camps were set up. The Beach Hotel in Marine Parade was used by senior officers for pre-invasion planning. After the large gatherings were over they would be seen coming from their meetings with brief cases and maps under their arms.

British and Canadian troops took over many streets of empty houses. Courtlands, now belonging to the Worthing Hospital Group, was a Canadian headquarters. The woods around Castle Goring on the road to Arundel were full of armoured vehicles.

In the early part of the year the British Commandos moved into the town and billeted with local families. Their HQ was in Broadwater Road next to the ex-Christian Science Church. This tough, highly trained body of men, lightly armed but able to travel fast in their jeep transport, could hit the enemy and withdraw, and were renowned and feared fighters. What a sight they made as they drove around the town with their green berets, combat jackets, coils of rope around their shoulders, all clutching sten guns! These men were among the first ashore on 6 June on that D-Day morning, sent in to capture gun emplacements. Less the killed and wounded, they were welcomed back to their Worthing billets when they returned to the town in August.

Keith Downer [6]

As Worthing was in a closed military area, wives were not allowed in the vicinity, although the Scots Greys' regimental history records that the ban 'did not prove to be totally effective'. [3]

Even honeymooners were caught in the regulations. Serviceman Derek Walker from Goring, who married a WAAF telephonist from the Durrington Radar Station, was refused formal permission to leave the area for time away together as all unnecessary movements were being stopped along the coast. [4]

The Scots Greys soon set about mobilising for battle by collecting new Sherman tanks and transport vehicles, arms and ammunition of all kinds, and absorbing reinforcements.

The brigade, part of the follow-up forces earmarked to land in the planned Normandy beach-head immediately after D-Day, was to remain in Worthing for almost four months. It left for Gosport on D-Day, embarking for Normandy the following day.

As might be imagined, a densely populated area such as Worthing hardly gave an ideal setting for the training of a brigade with well over 200 tanks and a considerably greater number of transport vehicles. Great difficulties in getting sufficient space were encountered. Some exercises used live ammunition 'not without an element of risk to the local inhabitants on their lawful occasions'. [5] Miraculously there were no casualties.

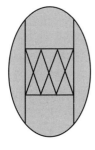

The Bolero Visitors

Towards the end of February 1944 the 30th US Infantry Division arrived in the Chichester-Bognor-Arundel area. This division, recruited in the Southern States, had only recently arrived in the United Kingdom under the Bolero programme. This was the programme for the build-up of American forces in the UK prior to D-Day. Crossing the Atlantic in troopships - forming part of the biggest convoy ever involved in the Bolero programme - the 30th Division had disembarked in Scotland and was at once sent south to Sussex for training.

30th US Infantry

Twenty years after the war, Frank W. Towers, the then President of the 30th Infantry Division Old Comrades Association, recalled that the division's 120th Infantry Regiment had been billeted in and around Bognor and Felpham between February and April 1944. He himself was billeted in a house called Suniyat in Summerley Lane in Felpham. He remembered the regiment's 3rd Battalion being

billeted 'on a point of land near the Channel's edge at Felpham..... east of Summerley Lane' and that the headquarters 'was in one of the down-town hotels, I believe the Victoria'. His recollections, published in the *Bognor Regis Post*, continued:

> I personally remember the wonderful hospitality of many of the residents....in Felpham, always calling some of us in as we were walking by for a pot of tea and a cheery visit. It was real heartwarming in those days for someone who had already undergone so much hardship to take time to care about us when we were so far away from home, some never to return. We who did return, however, have not forgotten this kindness.[7]

The giving of homely and friendly hospitality by West Sussex people was particularly valued by allied troops from overseas and is a constant feature in their recollections. In Chichester, Bishop Bell held receptions for American officers in the Bishops Palace to meet local people. Elsewhere in the city canteen facilities were opened for visiting troops such as in East Street and at Toc H premises in North Street.[8]

At Middleton-on-Sea a canteen was started by Mr. and Mrs. Vigur, affectionately known as 'Mom and Pop's Canteen'. It was situated on the site of what became the Candy Shop in Elmer.[9]

The scrapbooks compiled by Women's Institutes can be valuable sources on the war years. The Rustington volume continues the same theme of friendship:

> Many inhabitants offered hospitality in their own homes to the American and Canadian soldiers. The WVS ran a canteen at Moot House for them and the Land Girls, distributing hundreds of meat pies free of charge. The Hall proved invaluable for entertaining the troops occupying the village.[10]

Children often befriended the troops. Don Broughton was a teenager living in Westbourne during the D-Day build-up and had the enterprising idea of operating a fish and chip courier service to locally-based GIs.

> Around D-Day time there were many Americans stationed at Atchards which was down the path along by the stream and the Salvation Army hut. We boys had a good time with the Americans. They were confined to camp so we were given candy and chewing gum for going to the Westbourne fish and chip shop.[11]

On the negative side the potential damage to requisitioned property was a considerable cause of concern to local land and property owners throughout the whole war. More especially this was the case in the build-up to D-Day because of the sheer number of troops and the massive scale of their training exercises.

A considerable acreage of the Duke of Norfolk's estate covering Angmering, Burpham, Clapham and Patching fell within the South Downs Training Area, requisitioned by the War Office for intensive training. As such it was battered by tanks and other tracked vehicles and heavy military equipment. The 30th US Division manoeuvred on the Duke's property.

Requisitioning meant the ending of farming for the war years and the dispossession of occupiers. In the Duke's case it meant the loss of his race horse training gallops at Michelgrove. On Sunday 5

Wonderland

Sometime in the spring of 1944 we lads thought Christmas had arrived early. The army appeared and closed off half the [Crawley] Bypass, all the southern side, from the Tushmore roundabout to the bottom of Pease Pottage Hill, where Radio Mercury is now sited. Not only did they put up sentry boxes and a pole barrier at each roundabout access but they also built workshops for the R.E.M.E. (Royal Electrical and Mechanical Engineers). Some of the concrete bases are still to be seen to this day. The reason for this activity became apparent when dozens of tanks and armoured vehicles arrived to be double and treble parked on the road, cycle track and path and grass verge. There was still not enough room so the fields were used also. The fields opposite my home, now called 'The Dingle', were totally filled. It did not take us long to realise one young sentry could hardly supervise several hundred tanks.

5 Military Take-Over - Crawley Bypass

Churchill tanks wait silently along the bypass, May 1944.

When we climbed in through the hatch and lowered ourselves inside we were in a wonderland. The first thing to do was to adjust the periscope to keep an eye on the sentry. I believe we just looked about us without touching anything. The live shells were there for the gun. The cartridges all in place for the machine guns. A Colt revolver in a real leather holster. A Verey pistol and flares.

I was in a 'Churchill' one day and started the turret turning to the left....it was fascinating. I found the control and reversed it trying to peer through the periscope at the same time. As it slowly turned back, there he was, the sentry, racing straight towards me....I could have shot him I suppose, but decided instead to run for it. No doubt I left faster than if a member of the Wehrmacht had slipped a grenade through the driver's hatch, but it still took time. He caught up with me as I was about to climb over the fence into John Garman's garden; but do you know what? He hadn't thought of anything to say.

Rex Williams [12]

6 Military Take-Over - Crawley Bypass

Shrouded army carriers wait for orders to move, May 1944.

March 1944 he called a meeting at Arundel Castle attended by senior officers of a number of American Field Artillery units. He wanted to get some assurances for the protection of his newly-laid gallops, now confined to Arundel Park, as racing was to be kept going during the war as a deliberate government policy to keep up civilian morale and because of the vast capital value of British bloodstock.

7 Downland Battles
Bren gun carriers exercise on the South Downs near Arundel.

Compensation was paid for damage and loss of rents. Indeed the military authorities relied on the goodwill of local landowners, and the contribution of the major landed estates in the county to the D-Day preparations cannot be over-estimated. [13]

In the early months of 1944 American troops were arriving at the rate of 150,000 a month, bringing with them an average of 750,000 tons of supplies. The problem of finding suitable accommodation and training areas for such huge numbers was a major concern for Operation Overlord planners.

The 30th US Division remained in West Sussex until early April 1944. It was then

moved to Buckinghamshire to free the area for the British-Canadian build-up. The division later distinguished itself in a resolute stand against a major German counter-attack at the time of the break-out of General Bradley's 12th Army Group from the base of the Cherbourg peninsula.

Some American SOS - or Service of Supply units - remained in the Chichester area after the departure of the 30th Division. Residents of Bognor and Felpham recall a number of American servicemen involved in liaison duties at the Tangmere and Ford air bases, or on work on the Mulberry Harbour project, being billeted in the district. Some American personnel were also stationed in Selsey where there was a US Naval headquarters.

8 GI Take-Over
US troops unload their bunk beds as they prepare to take over homes 'in a South Coast village'. The military requisitioned houses and land for thousands of troops in West Sussex.

EARLY DAYS

9 **War On The Farm**
A farmer drives his flock of sheep past a stockpile of 500 pound bombs at a countryside Ordnance Depot, February 1944.

Unique Commando Base at Littlehampton

D-Day was still some nine months ahead when in September 1943 a highly secret and unique British army detachment, known to the few who knew of its existence at all, as X Troop of 10 Inter-Allied Commando, set up its base in Littlehampton.

In itself 10 Commando was a unit of a most unusual type. It was recruited mainly of volunteers from the free armed forces formed in Britain by exiles of the various Nazi-occupied countries of Europe. With a British manned headquarters, it consisted of soldiers from Belgium, Holland, Norway, Poland and France, plus X Troop.

Captain Bryan Hilton-Jones, an unconventional British officer, commanded X Troop. A brilliant linguist, he had secured a first class degree in modern languages at Cambridge, and reminded some people a little of Lawrence of Arabia. The membership of X Troop was composed mainly of volunteers of German origin, but with strong and proven anti-Nazi views, and of German speaking Eastern Europeans. Many were Jewish, or of partly Jewish extraction. Some had had hair-breadth escapes from the Gestapo before war broke out. Others were the sons of parents who had been living and working in Britain prior to 1939. Most had been interned as enemy aliens during the invasion scares of 1940. After vetting they were allowed to volunteer for the British Army, although at first only for non-combatant companies of the Pioneer Corps.

After this restriction was relaxed, and very carefully chosen volunteers were accepted for service in X Troop, its seventy-two members were each given completely new names and identities. Enemy recognition of their true origin, should any be captured, would almost certainly result in execution. Accordingly each man had to produce a carefully invented history, including false parents, civilian career and next-of-kin. For some reason all were supposed to have been members of The Royal Sussex Regiment, The Royal West Kent Regiment, The Buffs, and The Hampshire Regiment, whose cap badges they wore.

EARLY DAYS

The 10 Commando was never to fight as a unit, although its component troops all saw much action. After training in Wales and Scotland it was sent to Eastbourne early in 1943. In September the Dutch Troop was sent to the Far East, the Polish Troop to Italy, the Norwegian Troop to a Shetland base and its two French Troops to the Newhaven-Seaford area. The French were involved in several raids on the French coast during the winter, designed to confuse the German commanders about where the allied assault was likely to take place, and to gather information about enemy beach defences.

From its Littlehampton base, X Troop embarked on a programme of vigorous training. Captain Hilton-Jones had convinced his seniors that the only way to profit from the troop's linguistic and obvious intelligence-gathering abilities, as well as from what he described as 'the individualist temperament of members', was to employ it for specialised reconnaissance and small-scale raiding.

The commander of X Troop recorded that 'The nature of the countryside in Sussex gave ample scope for admirable training in map and compass work, fieldcraft [and] infiltration'. [14]

Under his direction the troop's programme covered bivouacking, abseiling, use of dinghies and dories and silenced weapons, night firing, parachute training, the use of homing pigeons, and endurance tests such as marching from the Black Rabbit near Arundel to Littlehampton in thirty-nine minutes. For a week the troop also carried out night exercises around Petworth, Midhurst, Steyning and Arundel, including a night-time reconnaissance of Arundel Castle.

In view of X Troop's close connection with intelligence duties it is not surprising that even today a considerable amount of mystery surrounds much of its operational work. Usually members appear to have been attached to other 10 Commando Troops or to other Commando units for specific operations. Five members, three of whom became casualties, took part in the Dieppe raid. Other members are known to have been attached to 10 Commando's French Troops which mounted the cross-Channel raids already mentioned.

10 **Commando Officers**
Captain Bryan Hilton-Jones,
whose daring X Troop
Commandos was based at
Littlehampton throughout
the build-up to D-Day,
is shown back row,
second from right.

Shortly before D-Day, there was an urgent need for more information about enemy beach defences. This was to involve one officer of X Troop in a most unusual and hazardous experience (recalled in Chapter 4). On and after D-Day all members of X Troop from the Littlehampton base were in continuous action, mainly on attachment to other Special Service units.

By the end of the war in Europe more than half the total strength of the troop had been killed or wounded. Publicly revealing the existence of X Troop for the first time, the former Commander of Combined Operations, Lord Louis Mountbatten, said in a speech in London in 1946 that 'They were fine soldiers and I was proud to command them'. [15]

EARLY DAYS

The Build-up Gets Under Way

Early March 1944 saw a steady flow of army units of all types into West Sussex. In the weeks ahead this rapidly became a flood. As ever increasing numbers of British troops moved in, Canadian units started to move out. The 3rd Canadian Infantry Division moved to Concentration Areas near the Solent ports. Other Canadians moved to Kent for Operation Fortitude. This was the major allied deception effort designed to convince the German High Command that a major concentration of military and naval forces was being made in the Dover area for an assault on the Pas de Calais coast, rather than Normandy.

11 Troops Pour Into Sussex

Thousands of troops took up temporary residence in West Sussex in the months leading up to D-Day. A sleepy village gives the backdrop to a British route march.

On 29 March the army headquarters of Sussex District issued a multi-page document headed 'Top Secret - Overlord, Administration Order No. 1'. The closely typed and highly detailed pages of this document reveal the enormous complexities to be faced in the build-up of massive numbers of fighting men, and members of the logistic services with vast quantities of war equipment.

Included in the document were instructions for the final laying out of Concentration and Marshalling Areas and points of embarkation, and for the provision of staff, construction and engineering facilities. Here too were details of the supply, transport, training, welfare, entertainment and postal arrangements, as well as essential medical and sanitation requirements. There was also information on security, air raid and fire-fighting precautions, data about wireless networks, right down to the supply of basics such as office equipment and stationery.

In addition to the possibility of enemy air raids designed to disrupt the build-up, possible enemy commando-type raids had also to be anticipated.

Some units were put on stand-by to deal with such a situation. The large number of airfields and landing grounds around Chichester was thought to be amongst the most likely targets of German commando attacks. The Home Guard was also on alert. West Sussex Sub-District headquarters ordered that all eight Home Guard battalion headquarters in the county should be manned on a

twenty-four hour basis for an instant call-out. As well as commando-type raids other dangers were considered to be sabotage by enemy agents dropped by parachute or brought in by small boat.

The Home Guard battalions were given such tasks as the guarding of bridges, railway tunnels and embarkation points. Each had to have 'in-lying pickets' available each night, ready to protect main traffic routes. They were also ordered to assist military police with the highly important task of traffic control. With so many thousands of military vehicles constantly on the roads, any major traffic jams could clearly throw tightly-knit movement schedules into complete chaos, as well as making ideal targets for prowling German aircraft.

Petworth Park's Armoured Assault Brigade

Few of the many thousands who visit Petworth House each year, or enjoy strolling in the peaceful expanses of its surrounding park, are probably aware that fifty years ago these grounds presented a very different scene. Petworth Park was then home to three camps with a combined capacity of 3,686 officers and men and several hundred vehicles.

Into these camps in the early days of April 1944, after a long journey from North-East Scotland, came the major portion of the 27th Armoured Brigade, a formation specially trained for beach assault operations. Their equipment included one of the major allied secrets of D-Day.

The brigade consisted of the distinguished regular armoured cavalry regiment, the 13/18th Royal Hussars (Queen Mary's Own), and two yeomanry regiments, the East Riding Yeomanry and the Staffordshire Yeomanry. Of these three, the first two were based at Petworth, whilst the third was *12* quartered at Wakehurst Place, Ardingly. All three were destined to play a vital part in the operations on the extreme left flank of the allied seaborne assault on D-Day. They were known as 'Water Assault Regiments' and had been trained in the use of the highly secret amphibious Sherman tanks, otherwise known as DD (Duplex Drive) tanks.

The Amphibious Sherman
DD Sherman tank with its inflatable canvas screen.

The idea that tanks could be adapted so that when launched from tank landing craft they could 'swim' to shore under their own power was the brain-child of a Hungarian-born engineer, Nicholas Straussler. After experiments had shown that the idea was feasible, and despite strong misgivings of naval experts, General Sir Alan Brooke, Chief of the Imperial General Staff, ordered the production of 900 DD Sherman tanks in July 1943.

DD Shermans were the normal Sherman tank - by 1944 the standard tank of the allied armies - converted to an amphibious role. A canvas screen, inflated by compressed air, was held in position by metal struts and compressed air 'pillars' around the hull. This screen formed a canvas 'box' around the

Sherman, increasing its volume in the water and allowing it to float. Two propellers in the rear provided mobility, the tank otherwise being driven in the usual way. Once the tank had grounded the propellers were raised, the canvas screen lowered, and it then moved forward on its track for normal operation.

All that was visible of the tank in the water was the top of the canvas screen protruding just above the turret, so making the vehicle a small target. DD Shermans seemed to offer a promising answer to one of the main lessons of the Dieppe raid. This was to ensure that assaulting infantry had sufficient armoured support to help them deal with powerful beach defences from the moment they left their landing craft.

Delays in production, however, resulted in there being far fewer DDs available on D-Day than the number ordered. From the 27th Armoured Brigade only two squadrons of the 13/18th Hussars were to go into action in them that morning. A number of accounts have praised what has been described as the `superb seamanship' of the crews in getting almost all their unwieldy craft to shore under weather conditions which were little short of appalling. Their success made a notable contribution to the rapid silencing of effective German opposition on Sword Beach, thereby saving many British lives.

An officer of the East Riding Yeomanry has left the following picture of his own regiment's pre D-Day stay in Petworth Park:

> The weather was almost too perfect for those six weeks at the end of April and all of May. The men were working stripped to the waist, and all were as brown as berries. For the 'Spearhead' all sorts of alterations had to be done to the tanks; we had to be completely equipped to live with what we could carry for two months except for food and petrol and ammunition. Special rods were welded, on which to clamp spare parts such as bogie wheels and springs to the tanks, for we never knew when spares could be brought up to us. The guns had to be `fired in' and tested, especially the 17-pounders....
>
> There was little time for recreation in those days, but there was a certain tense atmosphere of expectation; the days passed with incredible speed in perfect spring weather in a lovely part of England. In spite of feverish activity and increasing preparations, war seemed far away, except for the endless stream of aircraft preparing the way for us on the Continent. [16]

A stream of new vehicles and equipment now poured into Petworth Park and other Concentration Areas for the use of assault units. They came from huge depots such as those hastily created along the sides of the roadways on the Hogs Back and the Dorking bypass in Surrey.

CHAPTER 3

COUNT-DOWN

All through April and early May the build-up continued. In addition to the 27th Armoured Brigade the incoming flow into West Sussex included troops of two major formations soon to play a leading part in the front-line across the Channel.

Scotland in Sussex

By mid-April the major part of one of these units, the 15th Scottish Infantry Division, had arrived in West Sussex from Yorkshire. Made up of both regular and territorial battalions of well-known Highland and Lowland regiments it formed part of the 12th Corps which had been given the role of reinforcing the Normandy bridgehead as soon as possible after the D-Day landings. The 15th Scottish Division was to earn itself a fine reputation in some of the most severe fighting of the forthcoming campaign.

During its two month stay in the county the division's headquarters was at Knepp Castle, near West Grinstead. Its Lowland Brigade (the 44th) joined the 4th Armoured Brigade in Worthing, with headquarters in the Beach Hotel on the seafront. The Brigade's three battalions - the 8th Royal Scots, 6th Royal Scots Fusiliers and 7th King's Own Scottish Borderers - were also billeted in the town. One of the division's two Highland Brigades, the 227th, moved into one of the county's most ancient manor houses, Wiston, near Steyning. From here in the dark days after Dunkirk in 1940, Montgomery had directed the defence of the West Sussex coast. The 15th Scottish Division's artillery was spread between Ashington, Worthing and Lancing. Its engineers camped in Parham Park, near Storrington, whilst its 3rd Brigade, the 46th Highland, was billeted in Hove.

The division's historian has recorded that

> On arrival in Sussex the Division found to its satisfaction that its concentration area had
> that strongest of attractions to offer - comfortable quarters within reach of light
> entertainment. This fact, in combination with mild weather and a lovely countryside,
> persuaded even the critical Scotsmen to take a favourable view of their surroundings.
> Littlehampton, Worthing, Brighton and Hove were all within easy reach. There was still an
> air about these famous watering-places, shorn though they were of their peace-time glories
> and cluttered up with beach obstacles and barbed-wire.

13 **Knepp Castle**
15th Scottish Infantry
Division HQ.

COUNT-DOWN

Highland Light Infantry

It was something of a shock to find the tanks of the Guards Armoured Division in firm possession of Brighton's more fashionable thoroughfares. The harbours, too, on the Sussex coast were packed with a miscellany of multi-coloured landing craft, while overhead there passed an unending stream of aircraft formations gleaming in the sun. [1]

During its stay of nearly two months the division followed a balanced programme of work and play to keep it both physically and mentally fit. Sports fixtures included football against units of the neighbouring Guards Armoured Division camped just across the border in East Sussex. Exercises included one code-named Cow. In this exercise the three battalions of the 227th Highland Brigade living in tented camps - the 10th Highland Light Infantry at Wiston; the 2nd Argyll and Sutherland Highlanders at Cissbury, Findon; the 2nd Gordon Highlanders at Muntham Court, Findon - were deployed to follow up an artillery barrage in an imagined assault as part of 'battle inoculation'. Night exercises were also held on the South Downs Training Area, and the highlanders were constantly engaged on route marches, range practice, wireless training and mine-clearing practice.

14 **Wiston**
227th Highland Infantry Brigade,
15th Scottish Infantry
Division, HQ.

The perpetual difficulties of finding adequate training and billeting areas for the troops massing for Operation Overlord were dramatically demonstrated when three twenty-five pounder shells fired on a range at Steyning landed on the Highland Light Infantry camp at Wiston. Mercifully the damage was only to one rifle, one gasmask and two tents with only slight wounding to one soldier.

15 **Muntham Court**
2nd Battalion,
The Gordon Highlanders,
227th Highland Infantry Brigade,
tented camp was set up here.

Gordon Highlanders

16

As always with Scottish regiments, pipe and drum bands played a big part in the life of the battalions. On one occasion the combined pipe bands of the brigade played in a massed retreat for the brigade commander and his civilian guests. `Successful and impressive' went the report. [2]

Visitors to the division included the Bishop of Chichester who held a confirmation service, and Princess Mary, Colonel-in-Chief of the Royal Scots, who came to meet the 8th Battalion in Worthing. Some officers and men from the 227th Brigade's battalions took part in exchange visits with members of the 110th Regiment of the US Army stationed at Chiseldon in Wiltshire.

Some older residents still well remember the stay of the 15th Division. One has told of the unforgettable sight of the 10th Highland Light Infantry at Wiston marching off to war, headed by their pipes and drums, down the long avenue leading from the old house which has seen so many centuries of history. [3]

Wiston Highlanders

In mid-April 1944 my unit, the 10th Battalion The Highland Light Infantry, moved to Wiston Park near Steyning.

We were under canvas with brigade HQ in Wiston House. During the brief two months spent here we trained and enjoyed route marches through Sussex lanes in mainly sunny weather with the air above filled with planes. New kit, weapons and men arrived to bring the battalion up to full strength.

Jeeps, trucks, bren-carriers and anti-tank guns were waterproofed and final preparations made for the assault on Europe. Exactly when or where we did not know, but officers received a hard-backed book giving some details of Operation Overlord many weeks before the invasion.

I attended a short course in Cambridge on German defences on the French coast and the weapons they were using.

We did have some leisure time and I remember going to the Irish House in Brighton on more than one occasion for an enjoyable meal and a 'wee dram'.

Our training had been to break out of a bridgehead and exploit a breakthrough in combination with armour. When D-Day came we knew we would soon be on the move.

Early on 13 June the battalion split in two. Dressed in Full Marching Order the marching part of the battalion trooped to Steyning to take the train to a transit camp at Haywards Heath. On 17 June the troops were taken to Newhaven and embarked in a US and two UK LCI (Landing Craft, Infantry). I had missed the move because as a member of the brigadier's advance party we had gone to London on 11 June to board a merchant vessel to take us to Normandy. Unable to disembark because of rough seas we lay off the Normandy coast for a few days and then found the brigade had landed ahead of us.

Douglas Robinson [4]

General Hobart's Funnies

79th Armoured Division

Whilst the 15th Scottish Division was to play a leading role in the British 2nd Army's operations following D-Day, the 79th Armoured Division - established in its Advanced Headquarters at Muntham, near Barns Green in April - was to play a vital role on D-Day itself in keeping British casualties much lower than had been feared.

The division had been formed as a normal armoured division in the autumn of 1942, but in the following spring it was decided that all armoured and engineer units selected for a special beach assault role should be brought under its command. This was so that the development of new assault techniques would be driven forward under one senior officer.

The officer selected to command this unique formation was Major-General Sir Percy Hobart, a dedicated believer in the importance of tanks and other armoured vehicles in modern warfare. As commander of an experimental armoured force on Salisbury Plain as early as 1934 he had devised tactics which the German High Command subsequently adapted for its Blitzkrieg campaigns. Sent later to Egypt he formed the nucleus of what became the famous 7th Armoured Division, or 'Desert Rats'. But his radical views on the need for new tactics and equipment aroused the anger of the more conservative senior army officers and shortly after the outbreak of war he was prematurely retired. Indeed 1940 saw him as a corporal in the Home Guard! He was only recalled on the personal insistence of Churchill himself.

Although older than most World War Two field commanders he was an officer of immense energy and drive. He believed firmly that a prime need to ensure the success of the D-Day landings was to give the infantry the maximum possible armoured assistance for dealing with all types of enemy-laid beach defences and obstacles. For months before D-Day he is said to have driven an average of a 1,000 miles a week, visiting, advising and encouraging his widely scattered units training and experimenting with new or specially adapted armoured vehicles in secret training grounds in East Anglia, Wales and Scotland.

As well as supervising the development of DD tanks and the training of their crews, the division developed a wide range of innovative vehicles known as 'Hobart's Funnies'.

Hobart's Funnies

After the Dieppe disaster it was recognised that infantry assault troops must be preceded by armour specially adapted to deal with defensive obstacles. So were born the 'Funnies', the creation of Major-General Sir Percy Hobart, whose 79th Division arrived at Muntham and Barns Green near Horsham in April 1944.

16 **The Bobbin Tank**

The Bobbin could lay a ten feet wide canvas path for vehicles to cross soft sand.

These included the highly successful mine-clearing Sherman tanks called 'Crabs'. In front they carried a revolving drum from which heavy chains were suspended to beat the ground and explode harmlessly any mines in their path, so leaving a cleared track for following vehicles. Other Sherman tanks were fitted with a special mine-sweeping plough known as a 'Bulls horn'.

17 **The Crab Tank**
Revolving drums fitted
with lengths of chain for exploding mines.

Within the framework of the 79th Armoured Division was the 30th Armoured Brigade. This consisted of four armoured regiments equipped with Crab tanks, and two of its squadrons, one from the 22nd Dragoons, and one from the Lothians and Border Horse, joined the 27th Armoured Brigade in Petworth Park. The division also included the 1st Assault Brigade Royal Engineers, formed as a direct result of the lessons of the Dieppe raid. Its three regiments were equipped with various types of bridge-laying tanks, including tanks which could lay tracks to cover soft ground, or fill anti-tank ditches with bundles of metal rods making them easier to cross. There were tanks for carrying heavy mortars designed to pulverise pillboxes and concrete anti-tank obstacles, and a flamethrower fitted to a Churchill Mark VIII for burning out strongpoints, a weapon particularly feared by the Germans.

18 **The Bulls Horn Tank**
Giant fingers dig into
the sand to lift and
clear mines.

The great value of the operations of assault teams from the 79th Armoured Division on D-Day was indicated in a speech by Churchill to the House of Commons on the day of the landings. He declared that it seemed that the defences of Hitler's Fortress Europe had proved less insurmountable than expected, in no small part due to 'certain ingenious modifications' carried out on British tanks. [5]

Supreme Allied Commander in Chichester

On Wednesday 19 April General Eisenhower left Supreme Allied Expeditionary Force Headquarters at Bushy Park - code-named Widewing - for Chichester. Here he was to stay for three days in the Ship Hotel in North Street. Much of his time on this visit was spent in inspecting local airfields with the RAF's Air Chief Marshal Sir Arthur Tedder. On 20 April he

COUNT-DOWN

visited the Advanced Landing Ground at Apuldram.

Here three squadrons of the Free Czech Air Force of the RAF's 84 Group were currently stationed, equipped with modified Spitfires fitted with bomb-racks. That morning all three squadrons had taken part in a dive-bombing attack on a target south-east of Abbeville. Eisenhower was received by Air Chief Marshal Sir Trafford Leigh-Mallory, Commander of the Allied Expeditionary Air Force, and Air Marshal Sir Arthur Cunningham, Commander of the 2nd Tactical Air Force, and other senior officers. After lunch he addressed the airfield's assembled pilots and ground crew and then left for discussions in the air operations control centre set up in Bishop Otter College in Chichester. On D-Day the college was to be the nerve centre for the operation of fifty-six squadrons flying from airfields between Friston, near Eastbourne in the east, to Lee-on-Solent in the west, and northwards to Surrey and Berkshire.

19 Tangmere Dinner Seating Plan

On the evening of the following day - 21 April - the Allied Supreme Commander was the guest-of-honour at a formal dinner in the RAF officers' mess at Tangmere. The dinner was attended by nine Air Chief Marshals, Air Marshals and Air Vice-Marshals and fifty-two other senior officers involved in the air operations. They dined on *Filet de Boeuf A L'Americaine* and Christmas pudding.

ROYAL AIR FORCE, TANGMERE - THE SHIP HOTEL, CHICHESTER

Air Vice Marshal *Izycki*   Air Marshal *Sir R.M. Hill*   Group Capt. *A. G. Malan*   General *D. Eisenhower*   Air Chief Marshal *Sir Trafford Leigh-Mallory*   Air Chief Marshal *Sir Arthur W. Tedder*   Air Vice Marshal *H.W.L. Saunders*   Air Marshal *Sir Arthur Coningham*

Group Captain *Fenton*

Wing Commander *G.R.A. McJohnston*

Group Captain *J. Rankin*

Wing Commander *Stewart*

Wing Commander *Hampshire*

Group Captain *D.J. McBrien*

Wing Commander *Keefer*

Wing Commander *B. Drake*

Wing Commander *K. Alrazek*

Wing Commander *Berry*

Wing Commander *R.H. Thomas*

Wing Commander *P.R. Walker*

Air Commodore *Crosse*

Wing Commander *Harries*

Wing Commander *J.E. Johnson*

Group Captain *P. Davoud*

Wing Commander *R.P.T. Davidson*

Wing Commander *Chadburn*

Group Captain *Gillam*

Wing Commander *R.Baker*

Wing Commander *B. O'Brien-Hoare*

Wing Commander *R.P. Beaumont*

Wing Commander *Leathart*

Commandant *B. Du Perier*

Air Vice Marshal *L.O. Brown*

Air Vice Marshal *K. Janousek*

General *L. Brereton*

Air Vice Marshal *H. Broadhurst*

A dinner given to General D. Eisenhower on the occasion of his visit to Chichester when visiting troops preparing for the invasion of Europe. He stayed at THE SHIP HOTEL from Wednesday 19th April until Saturday 22nd April 1944.

Wing Commander *P.J. Simpson*

Group Captain *Gabszewicz*

Wing Commander *R. Marples*

Group Captain *Edge*

Lieutenant Colonel *R.A. Berg*

Group Captain *Jamieson*

Wing Commander *Maxwell*

Group Captain *Cunningham*

Wing Commander *Raphael*

Wing Commander *T. Vibiral*

Group Captain *Anderson*

Wing Commander *D. Scott*

Wing Commander *de Soomer*

Group Captain *W.J. Crisham*

Wing Commander *S. Skalski*

Group Captain *F. Rosier*

Wing Commander *J. Kowalski*

Wing Commander *Duke-Wooley*

Wing Commander *Scott-Malden*

Lieutenant Colonel *Birksted*

Wing Commander *L. Habjohn*

Wing Commander *Grice*

Wing Commander *A. Deere*

Squadron Leader *King*

Group Captain *Montcrieff*

Wing Commander *Green*

Squadron Leader *L.H. Farbrother*

Wing Commander *Wiggins*

20

COUNT-DOWN

Returning to Bushy Park on 22 April General Eisenhower told a member of his staff that as well as making a speech at the dinner he had also given seven talks to RAF personnel whilst on the trip. It had been 'interesting but wearing'. [6]

For the Supreme Commander the last few weeks had in fact proved a particularly stressful time. Serious disagreements had broken out - sometimes heated - between members of the allied high command. The arguments centred on whether the main weight of the allied bombing offensive should continue to be targeted on German industry or shifted to concentrate on smashing German transport facilities to hamper enemy supply lines to France. Eisenhower argued the case for interrupting the supply lines - and won.

20 **Tangmere Dinner -**
The Guest-of-Honour
General Eisenhower
(extreme left)
talks to Air Chief Marshal
Sir Trafford Leigh-Mallory,
Commander of the Allied
Expeditionary Air Force.

War on the Downs

Whilst the 27th Armoured Brigade, the 15th Scottish Infantry Division and many other units moved into West Sussex during April 1944, the 3rd Infantry Division - one of the two British D-Day assault divisions - had left its training ground in North-East Scotland for its Concentration Area in the woods of Hampshire. Lack of adequate training room there led to various units from the division coming to use the South Downs Training Area in West Sussex.

Ron Ham, who lives at Storrington, remembers that the Downs provided a very realistic training ground for both British and Canadian troops stationed in the area:

> From soon after the Dunkirk evacuation to the Normandy landings, gunfire and the
> screech and clatter of tank tracks became familiar sounds on the Downs and in the
> surrounding towns and villages. Once peaceful hilltops and farms were pounded by all
> types of ammunition fired from light and heavy artillery guns, trench mortars and machine
> guns, tanks and small arms. This all became more intense prior to D-Day. Continuous
> training gradually waned as the troops left to reinforce the armies fighting their way deeper
> into German occupied Europe. [7]

One of the ranges within the South Downs Training Area was at Kithurst Hill just outside Storrington, used by the 8th Infantry Brigade of the 3rd Division. This brigade was to lead the assault on Sword Beach on D-Day. The training schedule issued by brigade headquarters allocated the Kithurst range on a rotational basis to its three battalions: the 1st Battalion The Suffolk Regiment, the 2nd Battalion The East Yorkshire Regiment and the 1st Battalion The South Lancashire Regiment. All troops were to debuss at Houghton and then march to the range via Amberley Mount and Rackham Hill. Orders laid down that it was to be a 'forced march' and be covered in fifty minutes.

**3rd British Infantry
Division**

The Kithurst Hill military range was heavily used by a variety of units, some of them stationed nearby in Parham Park. Only recently, in November 1993, a Mark IV Churchill tank, used as a target here fifty years ago, was dug up from its resting place beneath a downland field. [8]

The wartime association of the 3rd Division with West Sussex extended far beyond the use of the South Downs Training Area. For much of the early summer of 1940, following its return from

21 **Tank Recovery 1993**
A Churchill tank used for target practice on the Kithurst range fifty years ago is excavated by Territorials of 118th Recovery Company, Royal Electrical and Mechanical Engineers, November 1993.

22 **Stansted Park**
Transit camp for Free French and Canadian units of the 3rd British Infantry Division.

Dunkirk, it had been responsible for coastal defences between Brighton and Bognor under the command of General Montgomery. Now, in the build-up to D-Day, it was briefly to return in full force to the same coast, but this time on a very different mission. It was to take part in the last major rehearsal exercise for the D-Day onslaught.

Landing Exercises

All through 1943 and the early months of 1944, British, Canadian and American assault forces had been training in landing exercises along the South Coast, some at Bracklesham Bay to the south of Chichester. The crews of landing craft rehearsed how to beach and unbeach. Tank crews learnt how to manoeuvre ashore, whilst thousands of allied troops practised assault procedures for the Normandy beaches. By no means were all the exercises successful. They demonstrated only too graphically that disaster could overtake the whole Overlord Operation if troops landed in the wrong place or in the wrong order, or if liaison between the naval, army and air force units failed to work effectively.

Maurice Henly, who served in the Civil Defence, Rescue Service and Fire Service at the time, can remember three landing exercises in Bracklesham Bay in the first few months of 1944. The largest involved a combined force of some 3,000 British and Canadian troops which had trained on the hills near Liphook and Petersfield. Embarking from Portsmouth and Hayling Island they landed on a beach two miles wide between Shore Road and East Bracklesham Drive, East Wittering. They were led by heavy tanks which dragged aside the concrete sea defences, followed by two of Hobart's

23 **Landing Exercises**
Exercises were staged at various locations along the West Sussex coastline during the build-up period. Here a group of LCTs (Landing Craft, Tank) prepare to hit the beach.
In the foreground engineers put down a slat and wire road for tank and truck traffic.
Barrage balloons complete the scene overhead.

Funnies - Crab tanks - which caused some havoc:

> One went via Shingle Walk. The other went via Legion Way. This one finished at Stubcroft Farm, about a quarter of a mile further inland. There were seven or more seafront bungalows demolished. They went straight ahead and everything in their path was destroyed. I heard afterwards those were their instructions - to turn sideways would present a better target for the enemy!

The Crab tanks were not alone in making their mark on the local scene. A flamethrower tank landed at the end of East Bracklesham Drive, near Earnley Marshes, destroying huts and everything else in its way.

The troops were brought in by approximately fifty landing craft, escorted by two destroyers and two frigates. A hospital ship moored off the Nab Tower. It was attacked by two Focke Wulf fighter-bombers but these were driven off by fighters from Tangmere and shot down over the Channel. The exercise produced about thirty fatalities. Some drowned when two landing barges collided and others were killed by undetected land mines on the beaches.

The whole operation lasted from 5.30 to 11 in the morning. The tanks and other vehicles afterwards made a rendezvous by the roadside in Birdham, and army trucks took the infantry back to base once they had cleared up and salvaged equipment stranded on the beach. The exercise was conducted under conditions of high security - all roads were patrolled by resident soldiers and the Home Guard, and all civilians had been ordered to remain indoors.[9]

Final Rehearsal

The last major assault rehearsal was code-named Exercise Fabius. It involved the whole of the British 1st Corps, namely the 3rd British and 3rd Canadian Infantry Divisions, and some commando and armoured units plus others under the direct command of the British 2nd Army. The exercise was based on a full assault landing on a stretch of `enemy' coastline running between Littlehampton and the eastern outskirts of Bognor. Similar landings were also practised at Bracklesham and Hayling Island.

24 **Landing Exercises**
Warships give an impressive backdrop as assault forces make their way ashore.

The 3rd British Division, led by the 8th Infantry Brigade, was supported by the Petworth Park based 27th Armoured Brigade, including the two squadrons of the 13/18th Hussars equipped with DD Sherman tanks. The division was also backed up by mine-clearing Crab tanks of the 22nd Dragoons, and by the special purpose tanks of the 5th Assault Regiment Royal Engineers, both from the 79th Armoured Division. It was to land in the area defined in the exercise plans as `Able Sector', better known to day trippers and holiday makers as Climping Beach.

25 **Exercise Fabius**
With landing craft in the background,
tanks and lorries of the 9th Canadian Brigade
come ashore at Bracklesham.

26 **Exercise Fabius**
A Churchill tank negotiates the sea wall
and coastal defences at Bracklesham.

The 8th Brigade was then to advance and 'capture' Yapton, moving northwards as far as the Ford-Barnham railway line. Meanwhile commandos of No. 41 (Royal Marine) Commando were to `mop-up' Littlehampton, and No. 4 Commando with the two French Troops of 10 Inter-Allied Commando, were similarly to 'mop-up' Middleton. The 27th Armoured Brigade was to advance over Arundel Bridge - assumed to have been `captured' by the 6th Airborne Division - and then to occupy Kithurst Hill.

All troops were warned about giving any details of tactics or equipment to outside persons. Any casualties taken to hospital must be kept free from contact with other patients. Once briefed for the exercise, troops were confined to camp and barred from using the telephone.

D-Day for Fabius was set for 4 May. The force sailed from Portsmouth and Southampton in perfect weather protected by a large `air umbrella'. Mercifully the landing craft were unmolested by the German E-boat flotilla which had attacked American forces only a few days earlier during an exercise at Slapton Sands in South Devon with the catastrophic loss of 749 lives.

27 **Exercise Fabius**
An army lorry of RE Company,
3rd Division, is driven off an
LCT (Landing Craft, Tank)
during the final D-Day invasion
rehearsal held at Bracklesham,
Climping and Hayling Island.

The landings at Climping went according to plan and a short but complicated `battle' then took place, the troops rehearsing the tactics they would be using in grim earnest in Normandy little more than a month later. Mock battle scenes engulfed well-known West Sussex locations from Climping northwards to Yapton and Barnham, up over the Downs to Bignor Hill, Chantry Hill near

Storrington, and Nore Hill near Slindon, reaching as far inland as Pulborough and Stopham.

These exercises were regarded as the most realistic way of testing the effectiveness of the combined forces, and they were studied carefully by the D-Day planners. It is said that the allied commanders, Eisenhower and Montgomery, together with the Prime Minister, Winston Churchill, watched the last of the landings at Bracklesham from the Bracklesham Bay Hotel. [10]

Recollections also refer to the presence of distinguished observers at Climping, including the Prime Minister again. A report by Dr. Hubert Lucking, a Middleton parish councillor at the time, suggests the importance of the occasion:

> A grand rehearsal of the Invasion
> scheme took place off the Elmer Coast;
> ambulances, W.V.S. Headquarters, and
> balloons were stationed off The Hard.
> Red Hats and Gold Braid took over the
> chief houses, and it was said that
> Churchill himself came to inspect the
> preparations. [11]

Civilian Hopes and Fears

By late April the civilian population of Southern England was increasingly aware that events of the most traumatic kind were upon them. One Worthing lady wrote in her diary of 'scenes of military and air activity' near Arundel and that 'the Downs near Worthing are almost all taken over by the military and are forbidden to the public'. A week later, on I May, she wrote: 'Everyone is keyed up to concert pitch over the invasion....We've thousands of the troops and vehicles in the town. We've got some of the 'Desert Rat' lorries here in Langton Rd, very decent Eighth Army men in charge. All Allied Expeditionary Force vehicles carry a large white, five pointed star.' [13]

At almost the same time another local resident, in Chichester this time, made the following entry in his diary: 'The whole world seems poised ready for the last "big do"....convoys of guns, tanks, lorries, ambulances....are common place.' [14] By the middle of May the Worthing diarist was writing, apparently somewhat impatiently: 'Still no invasion.' [15]

Climping Invasion

So close to D-Day, Exercise Fabius was quite a large gathering of landing craft and soldiery to get together as any enemy reconnaissance plane could have seen what was going on. But we never saw a German plane in daylight in those days and no doubt the RAF would have been out in force making sure the whole thing was not being seen.

I think we boarded at Warsash and sailed round between Bognor and Littlehampton, landing at about 9 a.m., more or less the same timing as on D-Day. I seem to remember it was a rather nice spring morning and the weather was calm, quite different from the real thing. The mines obviously had been cleared away from the landing area, as well as the steel anti-invasion obstacles, except, I think, those on the very top of the beach. I believe one of the DD tanks did hit a mine when moving up the beach on rehearsal. I suppose there was a certain amount of background effects put on in the form of smoke and explosions to make the whole thing rather more warlike.

I had been stationed in Littlehampton during the summer of 1943 and had exercised a lot in the area, so I knew exactly where I was. No. 6 Commando was to lead off the beaches on D-Day. No. 4 Commando had a specific job to attack some batteries to the west, so on this occasion I think they went off towards Middleton. No. 3 and No. 45 Commando were to follow No. 6 Commando inland.

Anyway, the landing was almost a dry one. I don't remember getting wet above the knees.

We speed-marched past Climping church, past Ford Airfield, over the railway line and on to the main bridge in Arundel. My troop turned right and kept on going to about Poling which had an RAF tracking station in those days. One of our troops had bicycles and they kept to the west of the Arun, past the Black Rabbit public house for a few miles. In fact, on D-Day, the bicycles were ditched as the ground was much too boggy for any of them to be carried inland for any distance. There were a lot of high-powered people watching the exercise, I believe. Certainly there were a lot of 6 Airborne about, as the 1st Commando Brigade was to link up with them on the Orne bridges.

Peter Cruden - No. 6 Commando, 1st Special Service Brigade [12]

'The waiting became intolerable for the British public, but the soldier knew better than to worry; it would come eventually, whether he willed it or not' wrote Sergeant H. Green of the 10th Highland Light Infantry based at Wiston. [16]

The public attitude towards the coming of D-Day was in fact somewhat ambivalent. On the one hand it was looked forward to as being an important stepping-stone towards victory and the end of the war. On the other hand there was the dread that it might produce casualty lists the length of those of the battle of the Somme in 1916, or even longer. This fear was not confined to ordinary civilians alone. To his closest advisers, Prime Minister Churchill made no secret of his bouts of trepidation about the possible losses.

There was also the apprehension that D-Day might bring the return of the Luftwaffe in force to home skies, a distinct possibility brought home to those living in Chichester just a few days after Eisenhower had left the Ship Hotel. Just after midnight on 25 April four high explosive bombs were dropped on Armadale Road, killing six and injuring thirty-one, causing extensive damage to property and entirely demolishing twelve houses. [17]

The Air Raid Precautions organisation - ARP - was mobilised and placed on alert all over the South to be ready for Luftwaffe attacks. But senior planners, both military and civilian, had far greater worries. For over a year now the fear haunting Overlord planners was that the enemy might be able to launch their secret weapon - known by the allies as Crossbow - to bombard Southern England and London before Overlord could strike.

For now aerial reconnaissance photographs showed that launch sites on the French coast for the first of these secret weapons - the V-1 or Flying Bomb - were nearly ready for operation. The race between the arrival of D-Day and the launching of the first Crossbow attacks was obviously going to be a very close thing indeed.

CHAPTER 4

POISED TO STRIKE

By early May there was little time left before Y-Day, or Halcyon, code-names for 1 June, the date by which it was ordered that all assault forces must be ready for action. It was forecast that over on the Normandy beaches the 5,6,7 June would produce the ideal conditions for D-Day - a rising tide at dawn, with moonlight the preceding night for the drop of airborne forces. After 7 June the same conditions would not be repeated for another fortnight.

28 **Burton Park**
Junior Officers' Mess,
1st Special Service Brigade.

The choice of the actual date for D-Day would largely depend on weather forecasts. For the minimum suitable conditions the seaborne force needed a sea no rougher than waves of three or four feet. The airborne force required winds no stronger than Force 3 (8-12 MPH). Weather in the Channel could usually be predicted only some forty-eight hours in advance.

Throughout most of May one fine sunny day succeeded another. West Sussex now contained the headquarters of two formations which, like the 27th Armoured Brigade, would be in the very forefront of the coming assault.

29 Lavington House
HQ of Major-General Sir Robert Sturges, 1st Special Service Brigade.
Now a school - Seaford College - it retains its commando links with
a small museum and an annual chapel service.

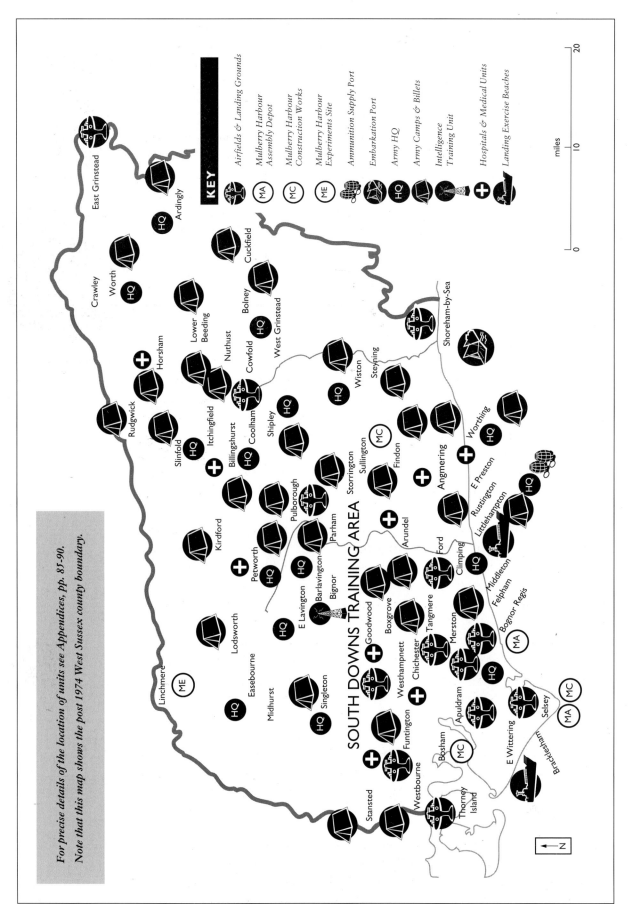

KEY

	Airfields & Landing Grounds
MA	Mulberry Harbour Assembly Depot
MC	Mulberry Harbour Construction Works
ME	Mulberry Harbour Experiments Site
	Ammunition Supply Port
	Embarkation Port
HQ	Army HQ
	Army Camps & Billets
	Intelligence Training Unit
+	Hospitals & Medical Units
	Landing Exercise Beaches

miles
0   10   20

For precise details of the location of units see Appendices, pp. 81-90.
Note that this map shows the post 1974 West Sussex county boundary.

SOUTH DOWNS TRAINING AREA

East Grinstead
Ardingly
Crawley
Worth
Cuckfield
Lower Beeding
Bolney
West Grinstead
Nuthust
Cowfold
Horsham
Rudgwick
Shoreham-by-Sea
Steyning
Wiston
Itchingfield
Slinfold
Billingshurst
Coolham
Shipley
Worthing
Kirdford
Storrington
Sullington
Findon
Angmering
E Preston
Petworth
Pulborough
Parham
Rustington
Lodsworth
Barlavington
Bignor
Arundel
Littlehampton
Linchmere
E Lavington
Ford
Middleton
Easebourne
Climping
Felpham
Midhurst
Goodwood
Boxgrove
Tangmere
Merston
Bognor Regis
Singleton
Westhampnett
Chichester
Apuldram
Selsey
Funtington
Bosham
E Wittering
Stansted
Westbourne
Bracklesham
Thorney Island

N ←

Map 1 *West Sussex D-Day Air and Army Units*

POISED TO STRIKE

Burton Park - now St. Michael's School - and Lavington House - now Seaford College - both near Petworth, were the headquarters of the 1st Special Service Brigade which had under its command Numbers 3,4,6 and 45 (Royal Marine) Commandos. In Cowdray Park, Midhurst, was the headquarters of the 4th Special Service Brigade, formed in 1943 for service in the Normandy campaign, consisting of Numbers 41, 46, 47 and 48 (Royal Marine) Commandos.

1st Special Service Brigade

Due to land hard on the heels of the assault forces were the Beach Groups. These included the 6th Beach Group, headquarters and elements of which were to be found in Petworth Park, and the 36th Beach Group, based in Chichester Barracks. The Beach Groups were made up of an infantry battalion with the task of securing the group's allotted beach in the immediate wake of the first assault, plus a number of specialist teams. These teams were provided by members of the Royal Engineers, Royal Army Service Corps, Royal Army Ordnance Corps, Pioneer Corps and the Military Police.

Beach Groups

Also included within the Beach Group's framework were RAF Balloon Sections, RAF Beach Sections and Naval commandos. Some units from all three found a temporary home in Petworth Park during the build-up.

RAF Balloon Sections were responsible for providing barrage balloon protection over the landing beaches against low-flying air attack. The RAF Beach Sections were to organise the landing of supplies and equipment for the construction of advanced landing grounds. Naval commandos assisted the Naval Beach Masters in directing the approach of newly-arriving vessels, allocating them the positions and order in which to berth.

It was anticipated that all Beach Group operations might have to be performed under heavy enemy shell fire, not only on D-Day but for some days afterwards, as indeed proved to be the case.

For the assault troops in the Concentration Areas, May 1944 was a mixture of last bouts of training, preparing equipment for action, officers' conferences, briefings for all ranks and then finally the sealing of their camps, effectively cutting them off from the outside world.

One of the most important tasks was the waterproofing of all armoured and transport vehicles for the beach landing. The task was far from simple. In 1944 the British Army alone had over one hundred different types of vehicle, many with their own highly individual waterproofing problems. One problem was how to protect vital electrical parts with a compound both easy to mould and heat-proof. For this an effective mixture of heavy grease and asbestos was devised. Engine air intake pipes had to be fitted with extensions protruding above any likely water level.

On 13 May General Eisenhower inspected the 27th Armoured Brigade in Petworth Park. In spite of his preoccupation with a multitude of intricate problems, the Supreme Commander was tireless in visiting his troops, gaining a reputation for informality and obvious sincerity. The brigade headquarters' war diary remarked that the 'General made a great impression and inspired tremendous confidence in all ranks'.[1]

Whilst A and B Squadrons of 13/18th Royal Hussars - chosen to fight in DD Sherman tanks on D-Day - had been hard at work ironing out teething troubles on newly arrived DDs down at Gosport, the East Riding Yeomanry had been 'shooting-in' its 75 mm tank guns and engaged in infantry-tank co-operation exercises with battalions of the 3rd Division's 9th Brigade which it was earmarked to

support on D-Day.

Petworth Park was now becoming a scene of steadily increasing activity with the many resident units employed in a wide variety of roles. The history of the 13/18th Royal Hussars refers to `waterproofing vehicles, the storing of innumerable loads of new equipment, and a seemingly endless amount of paperwork'. At the same time `there was also endless coming and going at all hours of staff officers and others from the most obscure units'. [2]

By mid-May the spearhead forces due to land in Normandy on D-Day and after had virtually all moved into their allotted Concentration Areas. This vast movement of over thirty divisions, each of 15,000 - 20,000 men and 3,000-3,500 vehicles, had remained largely undetected by the enemy. This was clearly revealed by a conversation on 15 May between Field Marshal Rommel, the German Army Commander, and a senior German naval adviser who lamented 'the lack of information with regard to the preparations in southern Britain, especially in and around the harbours, since our air reconnaissance had completely failed'.[3]

On that same day, 15 May, at St. Paul's School in London, General Montgomery was presenting the complete and final plans for the D-Day landings and the opening of the invasion campaign before King George VI, Winston Churchill, General Smuts, the Prime Minister of South Africa, and a large number of senior British, American and Canadian commanders. Using a huge relief model of Normandy showing the different types of terrain, and, where known, the German dispositions, he explained the plan of campaign. His address to the distinguished audience was rousing: `We shall have to send the soldiers into this party "seeing red". We must get them completely on their toes; having absolute faith in the plan; and imbued with infectious optimism and offensive eagerness. Nothing must stop them! If we send them into battle in this way - then we shall succeed.'[4]

Even as this historic meeting was breaking up, highly secret and urgent operations were about to try and discover information of considerable concern to the D-Day planners. These were operations in which several members of 10 Inter-Allied Commando's X Troop based at Littlehampton were to play a leading part.

An Extraordinary Meeting

In April a bomb from an allied aircraft attacking a target on the North French coast had fallen short and exploded in the sea. Immediately there was a series of explosions all along the foreshore from mines beneath the water.

The incident was reported to Professor J.D. Bernal, Experimental Scientific Adviser to Combined Operations Headquarters. He feared it indicated that the German beach defences now included a new and more powerful type of mine. If these did exist, and had been extensively planted, they could do great damage to the landing forces.

Accordingly, at the urgent request of General Montgomery, a special commando raiding force was put together at Dover for a reconnaissance of French beaches. Known as Hiltforce it was under the command of Captain Hilton-Jones, the officer commanding X Troop and second in command of 10 Commando.

The operation, carried out by carefully selected men from 10 Commando, including some from Littlehampton's X Troop, some officers from the Royal Engineers and other attached personnel,

was given the code-name Tarbrush. Eight raids were launched during the nights of 15/16 and 16/17 May. The four-man raiding parties were taken to points near the French coast in motor torpedo boats from which they transferred to powered dories and finally landed from rubber dinghies. They found no evidence of a new type of mine; it appeared that the chain of explosions had been of a 'sympathetic' nature. The firing pins of Teller mines - of a type already well known to the allies - had become ultra-sensitive through insufficient protection against sea water.

To make doubly sure, it was decided to go ahead with a further raid during the night of 17/18 May. The raiding party chosen for this was known as Tarbrush 10. It had already taken part in the raids of the two previous nights and was commanded by an officer from X Troop, Lieutenant George Lane, a former Hungarian Olympic water-polo champion who had been named Lanyi, and had come to Britain before the war as a student and subsequently worked as a journalist. His service with X Troop was via the Pioneer Corps, Grenadier Guards and Special Operations Executive (SOE) and he was the first member of the troop to be commissioned. Tarbrush 10 also included a Danish member of X Troop.

The story of their final raid has been related in much detail in Ian Dear's book *Ten Commando*. [5] The four-man raiding party, including Lieutenant Lane and an officer of the Royal Engineers, landed safely, but soon the approach of German patrols cut off the two officers from the rest of the party. The others waited in their motor torpedo boat with Captain Hilton-Jones until the early hours of the morning, but were forced to return to England without them.

Before long the two officers were captured and taken to the town of Cayeux. After several days of interrogation they were suddenly blindfolded and taken by car to Rommel's headquarters in the château of La Roche-Guyon. Here they had the extraordinary experience of being interviewed by the German commander himself.

Informed that he was about to meet 'an extremely important person' Lane was asked to behave 'like an officer and a gentleman'. He later told Ian Dear that he was then taken into 'a very beautiful, large room'. In it were the Field Marshal and several others including an interpreter. Rommel began the conversation in a somewhat ominous fashion: 'So you are one of those gangster commandos'. Lane replied that commandos were not gangsters but 'the best soldiers in the world'. This seemed to amuse Rommel and the interview then continued in quite a relaxed and friendly fashion, ending with Rommel promising Lane that he would be safe. Lane's companion was also seen by Rommel.

In all probability the Field Marshal's interest in the two saved their lives as Hitler had ordered that all captured commandos must be executed. They should have been turned over to the security service of the SS and would almost certainly have been shot. As it was they were sent to a prisoner-of-war camp.

Both Hilton-Jones and George Lane were awarded the Military Cross for their part in Tarbrush from which so much vital information about mines and other beach defences had been obtained.

Eve of Attack

Troops in the Concentration Areas scheduled to land on D-Day or its immediate aftermath now awaited the coded message 'Cornelius Plus' - the 'Plus' to be followed by a figure. This figure would give the number of days from the date of the message by which the unit must be ready, with all waterproofing complete and equipment loaded, to move at six hours notice to a Marshalling Area.

A special unit known as Build-Up Control (West) was not only responsible for handling the highly intricate task of co-ordinating troops into Marshalling Areas, and then subsequently Assembly Areas and embarkation points, but also for the movement and concentration of shipping.

In this waiting period much time was spent in studying the landing craft or landing ship loading tables. These could be extremely complicated documents. One ex-member of the East Riding Yeomanry has recalled that the table for his regiment, sailing in twenty-five different landing craft, came to twenty-one pages of closely-typed foolscap. He well remembered 'the fantastic amount of work required to settle the organisation of the assault - which vehicles went in what craft, how the craft was loaded, which vehicles went in first, according to the trim of the craft, all had to be worked out with the Navy and our Infantry, to the minutest detail.'[6]

30 **Wakehurst Place**
Home to
the Staffordshire Yeomanry,
27th Armoured Brigade,
April-May 1944.

On 17 May General Eisenhower sent the message 'Halcyon Plus 4' to the Anglo-American Chiefs of Staff in Washington, informing them that of the possible dates in early June he had chosen 5 June as most likely to provide the best conditions for launching the assault. He also decided to establish an Advance SHAEF Headquarters in the grounds of Southwick House, near Portsmouth. Montgomery had already established his 21st Army Group Headquarters not far away. The headquarters of two of the four British corps involved in Operation Overlord fell within West Sussex. The 8th Corps used Wakehurst Place at Ardingly, Worth Priory and The Grove at Worth, whilst the 30th Corps used Milton Mount College at Three Bridges.

Royal Army Medical Corps

Still no one except those very few already briefed and given the code-name Bigots knew the destination and objectives of the invasion force. The former BBC war correspondent, Chester Wilmot, wrote of this time in late May:

> For the men in the leading divisions these weeks were the severest test of morale. The listless air of uncertainty hung heavily over the camps and each day seemed longer than the day before.... After the middle of the month most of the assault troops had little to do but await the movement of the inexorable machine which had them in its grip. In its own good time the machine would move them down to the ships, across the Channel and on to the beaches. But which beaches? When?[7]

POISED TO STRIKE

At Goodwood House, near Chichester, extensive preparations were being made to care for the expected casualties. It was used by the 6th, 23rd and 121st General Hospitals Royal Army Medical Corps during the build-up period. The specialist and nursing staff occupying it now included two maxillo-facial surgical teams and a chest surgery team. There was also a base depot medical stores unit. A nurse based at Goodwood remembers packing hospital tents on the lawns and that these were later re-erected for advance medical facilities on the outskirts of Bayeux.[8]

In the Worthing area contingency plans were put into operation in anticipation of heavy casualties from the landings. Keith Downer recalls that a large field near Southways Avenue and West Street, Sompting, was laid out with huts and tents to receive wounded allied troops and captured Germans.[9]

On 22 May King George VI inspected the 27th Armoured Brigade in Petworth Park, an event enlivened by the 13/18th Hussars band from nearby Blackdown. The day was another brilliantly sunny one. In the full spring beauty of the park with the band playing, the King, in an armoured half-track, was driven along the ranks of the brigade drawn up in front of their spotless and gleaming vehicles. It was a memorable scene.

Royal Visit

George VI made pre-invasion tours of at least four camps in West Sussex and Hampshire on 22 May 1944. After visiting units of the British 3rd Infantry Division at Rowlands Castle he travelled to Petworth Park to inspect the 27th Armoured Brigade and Lord Lovat's Commandos.

31 **Inspecting Lord Lovat's Commandos**

32 **Inspecting 13/18th Royal Hussars**

33 **Inspecting Royal Electrical and Mechanical Engineers**

33

King Visits Petworth

I was a member of 11 Light Field Ambulance which gave mobile medical support to tanks in action. We moved into Petworth Park some weeks before D-Day with our brigade - the 27th Armoured Brigade. It was some 4,000-4,500 strong and our commander was Brigadier Prior-Palmer. The brigade's speciality was `Swimming Tanks' with inflatable hulls and extra large gun mountings on the tanks. We were the spearhead of the assault land forces.

We were successively inspected by Eisenhower, Montgomery and King George VI. The first two stayed at the old Swan Hotel in Petworth.

The King's inspection ended in anti-climax. He was, of course, pretty ill, and drove away after the inspection. Brigadier Prior-Palmer sensed the frustration - no one had illusions about the situation to be faced. He went to a hillock and told the troops to break ranks and gather around him. One wit saw the humour of this and bleated. Immediately 4,000 soldiers joined the bleating and became a flock of sheep!

We were deprived of most of our equipment which had gone down to the coast before us, so we had some leisure for a couple of weeks. We organised some cricket on the Petworth Park cricket pitch. It's amusing to recall that the Americans were playing baseball in the same area and their deep fielders were among our close fielders quite oblivious to our own game or the hard ball!

Jim Wheeler [10]

34 **The Task Ahead**
After the King had left Petworth Park, Brigadier Prior-Palmer, 27th Armoured Brigade, addresses his men on the task ahead.

POISED TO STRIKE

On the same occasion the King also inspected Lord Lovat's Commandos whose brigade headquarters was at Lavington House. At least one of his units, No. 45 (Royal Marine) Commando was based in the Petworth district.

The sun also shone brightly in Brighton two days later as the massed pipe and drum bands of the 15th Scottish Division played, marched and counter-marched at the Divisional Games. A young engineer won the piping competition, the 8th Royal Scots the tug-of-war, the 2nd Argyll and Sutherland Highlanders the three mile race and the foursome reel competition, whilst the 2nd Gordon Highlanders came second in throwing the hammer and the highland fling. The games ended with the massed bands giving those present a rousing send-off with a rendering of the divisional march *Scotland The Brave*. Just over one month later the division embarked on its first major action in bitter fighting along the river Odon in Normandy.

On 20 May senior officers from the 15th Scottish Division, the 27th Armoured Brigade and other units, had attended a map exercise in Chichester. At the end of the proceedings they had been addressed by General Montgomery. On 25 May it was the turn of General Eisenhower to visit the area once again. This time it was to inspect the 227th Highland Brigade at Washington, a few miles to the north of Worthing. After the inspection he asked the troops to break ranks and gather around as he made a short speech standing on the bonnet of a jeep. He considered himself privileged to have the 15th Scottish Division in `the great allied team' for the invasion. After these remarks he received three hearty cheers from his audience. [11]

Over in Normandy the sun shone brightly as well that day. Rommel, still with no real inkling of the advanced state of allied preparations, took the afternoon off to go rabbit shooting.

CHAPTER 5

AIR OFFENSIVE

Altogether some sixty squadrons of the RAF and British Dominion Airforces took part in the allied Overlord air offensive from West Sussex bases between January and the close of June 1944, operating with a total force of approximately 720 aircraft. In just one day in May 1944 a total of 730 offensive sorties were flown against targets in Northern France by aircraft from the Tangmere Sector alone.

At the outbreak of war in 1939 there were three military airfields in West Sussex, at Tangmere and Ford, and at Thorney Island on the Hampshire border. By early 1944 eleven airfields and advanced landing grounds were serving the needs of the RAF in the county.

Westhampnett, on the outskirts of Chichester - today used as a civil airfield called Goodwood - was the first of the additional wartime bases to be commissioned. As a satellite to Tangmere it played a crucial part in the Battle of Britain. Another satellite for Tangmere was Merston, also near Chichester, which became operational in 1941.

Tangmere played a particularly important part not only in the Battle of Britain, but in all air operations in Southern England throughout the war. As the controlling station of Sector A of the RAF's No. 11 Group it covered an area stretching from just west of Brighton to Bournemouth. After the fall of France in 1940 this was an area obviously very much in the front line.

In 1942 the Air Ministry began work on a plan to build a number of Advanced Landing Grounds - ALGs - along the South Coast to give improved air support for an allied expeditionary force landing in Northern France. Twenty-three were to be built in Kent, Sussex and Hampshire, and of these eleven were for the United States Air Force. Of the twelve allocated for British use, five were to be in West Sussex.

Land was requisitioned, but in some cases not without strong opposition from the Ministry of Agriculture and local farmers. Work on the ALGs by RAF, British Army and American airfield construction units began in December 1942. Each was to have a main runway of 4,800 feet and a second of 4,200 feet, with two Blister hangars and the possibility of a further two. The runways were constructed of various types of steel mesh track laid on the grass. Living quarters for both air and ground crew were usually meagre, mainly confined to tents, although locally some large houses were taken over as extra accommodation.

35 **'Sailor' Malan**
Group Captain
A.G. ('Sailor') Malan, DSO,
DFC, veteran of the Battle of
Britain, photographed at RAF
Tangmere. A former Merchant
Seaman, he sat at
General Eisenhower's right
during the famous
Tangmere dinner on
21 April 1944.

36 RAF Tangmere

Spitfire about to land with a tractor-drawn runway controller's caravan in the foreground, April 1944.

37 RAF Apuldram

Tented accommodation was normal, and not always very popular, at Advanced Landing Grounds, designed to give experience of operating from airfields with spartan facilities.

AIR OFFENSIVE

A few of the ALGs became operational in 1943, but in most cases they did not come into constant use until March or April 1944, subsequently making an invaluable contribution to both the pre and immediate post D-Day air offensive. After the allied landing and the big push towards Berlin most of the ALG sites were abandoned as the squadrons took up positions in France. 'They had served their purpose admirably and a large part of the aviation history of Sussex took place at them....Their concentrated short term use ensured them a place in the history books.' [1]

In West Sussex four of the five ALGs were in the Chichester area - at Apuldram, Bognor, Funtington and Selsey - with the fifth at Coolham, near Billingshurst.

At Apuldram three hundred acres of farmland were requisitioned and work on constructing the landing ground was underway by March 1943. Two metal-tracked runways were laid down, four Blister hangars built and tented accommodation put up for air and ground crews. The complicated arrangement of crossing runways, in the shape of a crucifix, with the main service road cutting across at two points, was made practical by a system of red and green signal lamps to prevent accidents. Initially Apuldram was the home of three squadrons of Typhoon fighter-bombers, but from 1 April 1944 it was to be base for three Czech Spitfire squadrons. In the build-up to the invasion they carried out raids on flying-bomb launch sites and road and rail targets. On D-Day itself its Spitfires gave cover to the British and Canadian landing forces in the Eastern Sector. Flying from first light until after dusk they carried out more sorties that day than any other RAF station. [2]

38 **RAF Apuldram**
Two of the Apuldram
Blister hangars, silent
and deserted after the war.

The ALG at Selsey took over land at Church Norton previously used as a private airfield in the 1930s. Two cross-over runways, the main one 4,200 feet long, the secondary one, 3,900 feet long, were laid down by an RAF construction unit early in 1943. Initially squadrons of Spitfires and

39 **RAF Apuldram**
Ground crew, June 1944.
Photograph from
the collection of
Squadron Leader Tony Liskutin
who flew from here on D-Day.

39

Typhoons were based here, and later Belgian and French airmen flew from here as well. On D-Day itself four squadrons of Free French Spitfires flew sorties over Arromanches. By March 1945 farmers were using the land again and today there is almost no visible sign of this wartime landing ground. [3]

The Aircraft

Of some sixty squadrons operating from out of West Sussex, thirty-eight were equipped with Spitfires, mostly with Mark IXs. Six other squadrons flew the American-made Mustang fighter-bomber, and thirteen flew Typhoons.

40 **RAF Apuldram**
Air and ground crew relax between sorties, June 1944.

The Typhoon was first produced as an interceptor fighter, but having been found unsuitable for this role was converted for ground attack, achieving great success with its rockets. When the Normandy campaign began, Typhoon-equipped squadrons responded to army requests for air strikes on enemy armour, often the only effective answer to German heavy tanks such as the Panther and Tiger.

Tangmere was base for a detachment of 161 (Special Duties) Squadron equipped with Lysanders for flying secret agents into occupied France on intelligence-gathering missions and to aid Resistance workers. French Resistance agents were sent to the Manor House at Bignor, a small village at the foot of the Downs near Pulborough. The house masqueraded as a convalescent home for wounded French officers but was really an undercover intelligence training unit for French men and women. The Manor's owner, Major Anthony Bertram, ran the house for three types of agents - for intelligence workers who gathered information about the enemy, radio operators who passed the information back to the British with a transmitter that fitted into a suitcase, and Resistance leaders. They were all trained to carry out incredibly risky work.

41 **Dominion Support**
Under the protective cover of an emergency hangar, Commonwealth ground crew work on a Spitfire.

They then flew from Tangmere, using Tangmere Cottage, opposite the airfield's main gates, as their secret local operations centre for many dramatic drops into enemy-held territory. The Lysanders could only operate when there was a full moon as the planes had to land in small fields, guided in by hand-held torches on the ground. [4]

The 277 Air Sea Rescue Squadron was stationed at Shoreham which was also base for No. 345 (Free French) Squadron of the RAF equipped with the modified VB type of Spitfire, a fighter-bomber with bomb racks and rockets.

The Airmen

Some thirty of the squadrons operating from West Sussex between January and the close of June 1944 were manned by British nationals. Six were Polish, two Belgian, three Czech, two Norwegian and four Free French. The British Dominions were represented by squadrons from Australia, Canada and New Zealand.

Strategy and Targets

Aircraft engaged in the pre D-Day air offensive from West Sussex were frequently involved in two types of operation known as 'Ramrods' and 'Rhubarbs'. The first were offensive sweeps by complete squadrons over particular targets in fine weather with the aim of eliminating enemy fighters from that area. 'Rhubarbs' were carried out when weather was unsuitable for major operations. Sorties of two fighters were given orders to attack 'targets of opportunity' seen on the ground. Attacks on the German flying-bomb launch sites - called 'No-ball' operations - were of high priority. Other prime targets included military headquarters, military traffic, airfields and coastal defences.

42 **Exercise 'Toughen-up'**
Air and ground crew had to 'rough it' while preparing for their part in the liberation of Europe: a Flying Officer's living tent on the edge of RAF Tangmere.

It was anticipated that the outcome of the post D-Day campaign would depend to a large extent on the speed with which each side could bring in reinforcements to the fighting zone. Lieutenant-General Sir Frederick Morgan, head of the COSSAC planning team, recalled in his memoirs that an American Civil War general remarked that in war the commander wins who 'gets thar fustest with the mostest'. [5] To make sure it was not the Germans who reached the Normandy battle front 'fustest' with the 'mostest', much of the allied air offensive concentrated on the French communications system, such as railways and road bridges.

In one typical attack the Czech-manned and Spitfire-equipped 310, 312 and 313 RAF Squadrons based at Apuldram successfully attacked a German armoured train and eight other trains near St. Malo in Brittany. During May 1944 the three squadrons of this Czech Wing flew a combined total of 1,521 hours.

Typhoon squadrons achieved a considerable reputation as 'train busters'. Even by the end of 1943 as many as 150 trains a month were reportedly being destroyed. Railway marshalling yards were favourite targets for attack.

43 **RAF Ford**
Spitfire Mission
Spitfire about to take off at
Ford for operations against
enemy air and rail targets
before D-Day.

As D-Day drew nearer the tempo of the allied air effort increased. Tangmere Sector log for 21 May reported a 'very busy day with aircraft attacking trains from Cherbourg to Boulogne. 5 locomotives destroyed and 28 damaged'. [6] Since early April Tangmere was the base for six Spitfire squadrons of the Royal Canadian Air Force which had attacked many road and rail targets during repeated sweeps over France. On 22 May 416 Squadron (City of Oshawa) distinguished itself by destroying four trains and then shooting down five enemy Focke Wulf 190s.

44 Ford Briefing
British and Commonwealth Spitfire pilots during operations against enemy targets before D-Day.

Mustang squadrons such as 19, 65 and 122 Squadrons at Ford, and later at Funtington, were able to penetrate even deeper into occupied Europe than the Spitfires and Typhoons. On at least one occasion 122 Squadron engaged on a Ranger operation flew almost as far as the Swiss border from Ford.

For over two months the Coolham Advanced Landing Ground was base for a mixed Polish and British Mustang Wing made up of two Polish squadrons, 306 (Torun) and 315 (Deblin), and 129 (Mysore) Squadron of the RAF. All three carried out a variety of operations, including deep penetration raids in late May 1944. Spitfire squadrons later based at Coolham included a Free Belgian Squadron (349) and a Royal New Zealand Air Force Squadron (485). [7]

45 Australians at Ford
Pilots of 453 Australian Spitfire squadron being briefed, May 1944.

The West Sussex Advanced Landing Ground serving the largest number of squadrons was Funtington. Twenty-six squadrons were based here for periods varying between a few days and several weeks between April and early August 1944. [8] For a short period in early May of this same year Funtington was base for a wing of Canadian Spitfires led by the famous `Johnnie' Johnson. With a total of thirty-eight enemy aircraft shot down he was the highest scoring allied fighter ace in the war.

During the run-up to D-Day and afterwards the Luftwaffe was greatly outnumbered by allied aircraft; most dog-fights seem to have ended in allied victory. Even so, sophisticated and efficient German anti-aircraft defences in Northern France exacted a considerable price from the attacking allies. The Tangmere Sector log records that in just one day towards the end of May the Sector lost nineteen aircraft `having to fly through heavy flack at low altitudes'. [9] After the war a memorial was erected near Falaise to the memory of the 120 Typhoon pilots lost over Normandy.

Bishop Otter College

On 15 February 1944 the RAF's Tangmere Sector Operations Room was transferred from St. James' Road School, Chichester - where it had been located since the bombing of Tangmere in 1940 - to the College hall at Bishop Otter College, less than a mile away. Here a special observation gallery was erected from which senior officers could look down on two large plotting tables surrounded by desks and a squadron-readiness board indicating availability for duty.

The plotting tables were manned day and night by specially trained WAAFs, divided into four watches of about thirty, each supervised by a WAAF and an RAF sergeant. Each watch worked a four hour shift in the day, and an eight hour shift at night. [10]

The role of this Operations Room is succinctly described in the words of a commemorative plaque installed here shortly after the war. At present hidden behind wooden panelling, the plaque is inscribed:

> The hall was extensively used during the preparatory phase before the invasion of Normandy to control aircraft on escort duties, intruder operations, attacks on transport and lines of communication, aerodromes and flying bomb sites and other tactical targets. During the invasion of Normandy, which began on 6th June 1944, fifty six squadrons taking part in the invasion were controlled from this room.

46, 47
RAF Tangmere Sector Operations Room Bishop Otter College
Artistic impressions by WAAF telephonist Elisa Blacker, 1944.

The Operations Room was fully staffed until the end of 1944, and then from January to May 1945 was maintained as an Emergency Operations Room with a reduced staff, directing fighter aircraft intercepting flying-bombs crossing the English coast. [11]

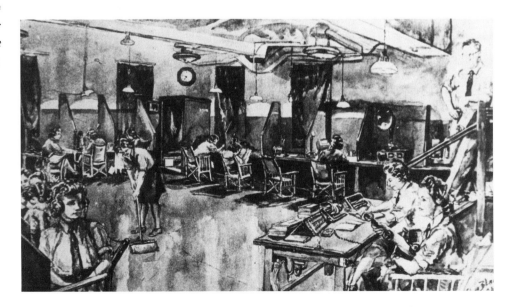

Bomber Tracks

On the long night watch I sit and think of you,
And when I see the bombers coming back
I pray that one of them is yours and bless
The arrows of each safely homing track.

(I hear you drumming through the night-dark sky
Another journey past, a journey done,
Another day ahead to live and laugh,
To eat, and sleep, and linger in the sun.)

The tracks move up the table, cross the coast,
The Filter Room, the plotters do their part -
But no one sees those wings beside your wings -
What symbols could they use to plot my heart?

**Poem by WAAF Corporal Helen Finch from the
RAF's in-house magazine when stationed at Bishop Otter.** [12]

CHAPTER 6

MULBERRY MIRACLE

Chicago Scene at Selsey

In the opening months of 1944 there can have been few areas of West Sussex where the civilian population was more directly affected by the war than Selsey. Raids by enemy aircraft continued, an all too frequent experience of the last three years, leaving a trail of damage and destruction. No fewer than thirty-one air raids were recorded for Selsey in the log kept by the Sussex Police Force during the war. [1]

Life in such a front-line area was governed by security regulations of exceptional strictness. From January onwards no visitors were allowed to enter the village unless they were service men home on leave, or had business of national or other exceptional importance. Residents were issued with special passes, and were forbidden to enter the Park - Pagham Harbour area. The sea near it was closed to fishermen. In an arc around the north-east corner of Selsey and Church Norton the Royal Artillery set up several batteries of heavy anti-aircraft guns.

From the village mysterious work on giant structures getting larger and larger each day could be seen rising out of the water. [2] By the beginning of June so many concrete blocks of various shapes and sizes had appeared that in the words of one war correspondent it `looked as if someone had picked up Chicago and put it down on the Sussex foreshore'. [3]

Even after most of these strange structures had been quietly towed away by an armada of tugs in the immediate aftermath of D-Day, it was still some time before local people became aware that Selsey had been one of the main assembly sites for two of the artificial harbours for the invasion of Normandy. Through one of these prefabricated harbours the British 21st Army Group received some forty-five per cent of its essential supplies.

48 Mystery Structures, Selsey
Huge concrete structures - Phoenix caissons - take shape off Selsey to be towed to France
for the Mulberry Harbour project. Top secret, locals could only speculate on their purpose.
In the foreground troops carry timber to an emergency landing pier being built in the
deep water channel near the end of Park Lane, Selsey, 1944.

'Don't argue the matter'

The failure of the Dieppe raid had alerted D-Day planners to the potential consequences of attempting to seize a heavily defended port in the first assault wave. Not only would it probably result in unacceptably heavy casualties but also in severe damage to harbour facilities, rendering the port ineffective for landing supplies.

The Operation Overlord planners were faced with formidable problems in ensuring a secure system of supply lines for the invading force.

It was estimated that every British soldier would require daily supplies of 20 lbs., and every American soldier 30 lbs., to support them in action. Every division would require 600 tons of supplies a day. Five divisions would land on D-Day and in the period immediately afterwards the number ashore would soon rise to over twice that figure.

The Normandy coastline chosen for the assault - nearly fifty miles long - offered little help. The harbours were very small, and in any case might be badly damaged. Unloading directly on to beaches presented particular difficulties because of the exceptionally large rise and fall of the tides. There were few natural havens to protect shipping from bad weather. In the case of a severe storm some 4,000 allied small craft would be in grave peril. In addition an Admiralty report had bleakly warned that `nothing favoured the choice of this coast for the construction of artificial harbours'. [4]

The idea of artificial harbours had first come to Winston Churchill when he was First Lord of the Admiralty in the First World War. Early in 1942 the same idea returned to him and gave rise in May of that year to his famous minute to Lord Louis Mountbatten, Chief of Combined Operations, on 'Piers for Use on Beaches'. He wrote:

> They <u>must</u> float up & down w[ith] the tide. The anchor problem must be mastered..... Let me have the best solution worked out. Don't argue the matter. The difficulties will argue for themselves. [5]

The Plan

By early 1943 the general concept of an artificial harbour, code-named Mulberry, had been produced under the direction of Vice-Admiral Hughes-Hallet. For the first time in history an invading army was to take its own harbour to an enemy-held shore.

The plan was to create a substantial area of water shielded from the swells of the Channel using a system of artificial breakwaters in front of Arromanches, near the centre of the sector where the invading troops would land. The area of calm water so enclosed would accommodate deep-draught ships and include quays for the unloading of supplies and jetties to link with dry land. The components would be prefabricated in sections in Britain and then towed across the hundred mile wide Channel commencing on D-Day + 1. The artificial port was expected to be fully operational fifteen days after the landing of the troops and to have a minimum lifespan of ninety days.

The design and construction of the three essential elements - the breakwaters, quays and jetties - presented considerable and complex problems: scientific, engineering and logistical.

The responsibility for the solving of key problems in one centrally important area of the project was to fall on the shoulders of a young Admiralty scientist from West Sussex.

47

MULBERRY MIRACLE

The Lilo Solution

Some of the enormous technical problems to transform the Mulberry concept into reality were handed over to the Admiralty's Directorate of Miscellaneous Weapon Development - DMWD. One of the leading members of this team, affectionately known as the Wheezers and Dodgers, was Lieutenant-Commander Robert Lochner, RNVR, whose home was at Rats Castle at Hammer in the parish of Linchmere, just inside the West Sussex county boundary. Events showed that he was to make a vital contribution to the realisation of the Mulberry Harbours.

Commander Lochner, an electrical engineer in civilian life, and a keen yachtsman, had joined the Navy on the outbreak of war. Before coming to the DMWD he had served in Coastal Forces. The particular problem on which he now focused his attention was how to construct an effective outer breakwater for the Mulberry. Working on the theory that waves only exerted their force over a comparatively shallow depth of water, he came to consider that what was needed was a floating sea-wall. Such a wall need not extend to a very great depth, but only to that at which the energy of the waves was exhausted.

49 **Rats Castle**

*Rats Castle at Hammer,
home of Lieutenant-Commander
Robert Lochner, RNVR,
major inspiration behind the
success of the Mulberry project.*

The germination of the idea owed much to a remarkable sequence of unusual experiments carried out at Rats Castle itself. Relaxing in his bath, Commander Lochner noticed the effect of his bag-type flannel in calming the ripples of the water. He then went from the bath to his trout pond in the garden. His wife Mary sewed a metal keel onto the family lilo which he floated in the pond whilst Mary simulated the motion of waves with the help of a cricket bat. The Rats Castle experiments gave the Commander his first practical proof that the theory was sound and that the force of waves could be suppressed by a floating barrier.

Mary Lochner recalls that her husband immediately returned to the Admiralty, spending much time away from home developing and perfecting the idea of a floating breakwater, overseeing a series of more sophisticated experiments. She remembers this as a time of great excitement and total secrecy, with many subterfuges and false expeditions set up in Kent and the New Forest. Such was the security that Commander Lochner and his team of scientists lived and worked in huts guarded by US sentries for some two months. [6]

50 **Lilo Experiment**

*Commander Lochner
experiments with a cut-down lilo
on his garden pond at
Rats Castle during early
work on the outer breakwater.*

A new code-word started to appear in the progress reports received by Overlord planners. The research work on the floating sea wall was officially given the title Lilo. At first Lochner and his team worked on an idea involving the use of gigantic rubber airbags with keels made of hollow tubes of

48

51 The Huts

US sentry guards the secret huts where Commander Lochner and his team of scientists lived for two months when working on the outer breakwater plans.

reinforced concrete. Three full-sized lilos, each 200 feet long and 12 feet wide, were under construction at Portsmouth during August 1943.

Commander Lochner still had a nagging feeling that the basic design might be improved as he worried over the possible fragility of the fabric sides of the breakwater being built. He continued to experiment, often in his bath, now with model barriers with rigid sides.

In August 1943, Lochner and four of his colleagues were summoned to attend the Quadrant Conference in Quebec with Churchill to consider the problems of Operation Overlord. The discussions were then moved to Washington. Here the Commander was summoned to give a twenty minute talk to President Roosevelt and Prime Minister Churchill on his theories.

52 Swell Data

Commander Lochner at work in his secret hut with graphs recording the amount of swell on the floating breakwater.

In addition to the Arromanches harbour for serving the British invasion forces in the Eastern Sector, it was now planned that there was to be a second harbour at St. Laurent-sur-Mer to serve the American forces in the Western Sector. Both should be capable of handling 12,000 tons of stores and 2,500 vehicles daily, and the components for both were to be a British responsibility. On returning to England the Lilo team learnt that experiments with a rigid-sided outer breakwater, carried on in their absence, had achieved a much greater success than expected.

The Anglo-American Combined Chiefs of Staff now laid down that the Mulberry's outer breakwaters must be capable of withstanding winds of up to Force 6 (25-31 MPH) and must be able to give some measure of protection to shipping by D-Day +4. In mid-September, with only seven months to go before what was then the target date for D-Day, 1 May 1944, it was decided to concentrate on what recent experiments had shown to be feasible: a steel barrier designed to translate the thrust of the waves into a vertical motion comparatively devoid of much force. Initially this improved version was called Hard Lilo to distinguish it from the original idea of a rubber and concrete structure. Subsequently it was code-named Bombardon.

53 **How it Works**
Commander Lochner (left) discusses the floating breakwater with Rear-Admiral W.R. Patterson, CB, CVO, ACNS (middle).

Before any work could start on the construction of such a breakwater, over 300 experiments had to be carried out with scale models. Many were carried out in a water tank at Haslar at Gosport where a complete model of a Mulberry harbour was built.

To get as much information as possible about the behaviour of waves, Commander Lochner set up an observation post with special recording instruments in the care of a reliable DMWD Wren, a petty-officer based in a Newhaven lighthouse. Meanwhile Lochner and some of his colleagues spent time on cliffs in the area timing the duration of waves and collecting as much information as possible for future analysis.

54 **Phoenix Caisson, Selsey**
The Mulberry Harbour project required the construction of 150 huge concrete caissons. Here a tug tows a caisson off Selsey.

The Bombardon breakwaters were to be made up of hollow steel caissons in the shape of Maltese Crosses, each 200 feet long by twenty-five feet wide with a draught of nineteen feet, and each containing buoyancy chambers. There were to be two parallel lines of Bombardons, 800 feet apart, acting as a double barrage to reduce the energy of the waves to one-tenth their original strength. Ninety-six units were to be built, in sections, for the two Mulberries. The work employed 1,700 men at Tilbury and Southampton for six months and used over 25,000 tons of steel.

MULBERRY MIRACLE

Final experiments were now transferred to Weymouth Bay in Dorset. In the first two days of April the Bombardons adequately withstood an inshore gale gusting up to Force 8 with waves eight feet high and 200 feet long for ten hours, giving conditions of stress twice as great as the barrier had been designed to meet. [7]

While the final tests and development of the outer breakwater continued, work was also being completed on all the other Mulberry components at the two main assembly depots at Dungeness and Selsey.

Behind the outer Bombardon breakwater an inner breakwater was planned to be made up of a line of scuttled ships to make the so-called Gooseberry breakwaters, extended and braced by huge concrete caissons - the Phoenix caissons. The largest of these would measure over 200 feet long by forty feet wide with a height of some sixty feet and would weigh up to 6,000 tons. In all 15,000 men worked on their construction using 630,000 tons of concrete. The object was to form a solid barrage some two miles long parallel to the coast about one mile offshore. The barrage would be flanked at each end by further breakwaters at right angles to the shore, thereby giving greater protection to the harbours.

In the centre of the harbours it was planned to install loading quays called Whales. These were floating platforms made up of unsinkable caissons, sliding up and down steel piles with the tides. These were to be connected to floating metal roadways to the shore. [8]

♪♪ **Floating Jetties**
Jetties provided floating metal roadways to connect with the shore.
The Selsey Mulberry assembly site is in the background.

The building of all the many components for this massive project necessitated a huge construction programme. Whilst much was concentrated in a number of main depots, other work was carried out in creeks and inlets around the coast, and by specialist firms inland. Local people recall construction work carried out at Burne's shipyard at Bosham. Blocks of concrete, remnants of the project, can still be seen along the east side of Bosham Channel. [9] Work was also undertaken at Sullington, near Storrington, by the Marley Tile Company. [10]

As well as the gigantic construction operation, the actual deployment of the artificial harbours meant facing other urgent measures of quite a different type. What was essential was to gather the maximum possible topographical and hydrographical information about the Normandy coast. Not much up to date information was available, existing charts being based on the last French survey of 1836. A large scale photographic operation had to be made by a squadron of Spitfires, unarmed and stripped of all non-essentials to increase their speed and range in surveying over sixty-five miles of coastline, at all states of tide, weather and light.

MULBERRY MIRACLE

The operation was complicated by the fact that repeated visits by reconnaissance planes concentrating on one area alone would have alerted the Germans to the target area, so decoy photo-reconnaissance flights had to be made all along the coast of occupied Europe. These official photographs supplemented other pictures taken along the French coast by civilians in peace time: the BBC had appealed to listeners to send in their holiday snaps and eventually the survey teams were to receive over ten million views.

Information that could not be adequately gained by photography had to be gathered by other means. Six weeks before D-Day one naval officer carried out a full survey of the Arromanches area in a small boat from which he took soundings. Peter Cruden, serving with No. 6 Commando, 1st Special Service Brigade, remembers that the Special Boat Squadron had units in and around Bognor prior to D-Day, sending over small parties of soil experts and engineers to measure tides and collect other vital data from the landing beach areas.[11]

The Greatest Towing Operation in History

At Selsey and the other assembly points along the coast the extraordinary sight of giant structures of concrete and steel rising out of the water fuelled rumour and speculation. The socialite Lady Diana Cooper returned to West House, her holiday home at the sea end of Barrack Lane in Aldwick near Bognor, just before D-Day. She recalled

> the sea-verge....like a redoubtable barbican, now....an area barred to non-residents....
> most surprising, there were Mulberries floating at some distance from my garden wall.
> The townspeople and locals noticed them no longer, and would say if you asked their
> purpose that they thought they were some submarine defence....There were other
> explanations for them....None of them tallied with one another. The English were by
> then used to cover-stories, and accepted ignorance with relief.[12]

The mysterious floating blocks riding the waves were the best kept secrets of the war. Bognor people said they were a new type of prefabricated building for the town's new housing estate. At Bosham they were saying it was the start of a concrete bridge to cross the Channel![13]

Relics of these Mulberry harbours can still be seen today, wrecked in the sea off Aldwick and Pagham. Rough weather upset the practice assembly of the Mulberry units, parts broke loose and were abandoned. At least four sections were lost; one lies submerged off Pagham Harbour, another is embedded in the sand on the Aldwick foreshore. When it was first washed up local children remember scrambling all over its deck. The same storm which brought in this pontoon also washed in a huge metal cylindrical float, a heavy caisson some thirty feet long, seven in diameter, which drifted eastwards demolishing groynes in its path until coming to rest near the east end of what is now Marine Drive West where it was cut up and cleared away.[14]

Command of the awesome task of hauling one million tons of concrete, 50,000 tons of steelwork, six miles of piers and 120 miles of steel cables over to the Normandy coast for the two Mulberries was assigned to Rear-Admiral William Tennant who had played a major part in the Dunkirk evacuation in 1940.

The cross-Channel procedure started with the departure of the doomed blockships to be scuttled at the end of the journey as part of the inner breakwater system. They went a few hours after the initial landings and on the next day floating rafts were towed over carrying the various Mulberry

components to their allotted stations. A fleet of some 140 tugs was amongst the many different types of vessels used. Less than a week after the towing operation began, and despite enemy shell fire, the artificial harbours had disembarked 74,000 troops, 10,000 vehicles and 17,000 tons of weapons, food and fuel.

56 **Bognor's D-Day Relic**
Wrecked Mulberry unit photographed on West Beach, Aldwick, in February 1965.

The great summer solstice storm of 19-22 June, with north-easterly winds in the Channel gusting to Force 6-7, wrecked the American harbour at St. Laurent-sur-Mer. Although the Arromanches harbour was damaged, and some equipment had been lost in transit at sea, the port had shown considerable resistance to the storm and by mid-July 6,000 tons of supplies a day were being unloaded.

A number of the Mulberry installations still survive at Arromanches where they can be seen quite clearly just off the shore. The full story of the Mulberry operation here is vividly illustrated in the Musée du Débarquement (Invasion Museum) in the little seaside resort. 15

57 **Arromanches**
A floating jetty is manoeuvred into place, June 1944.

58 **Arromanches**
A buckled pier-head road photographed after the great summer storm of 19-22 June 1944.

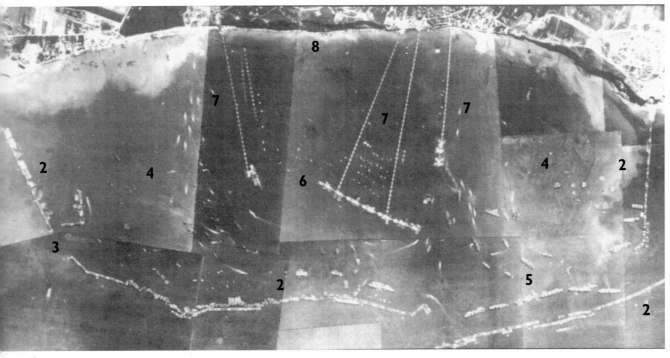

I ×××××××××××××××××××××××× I

59 **Mulberry: a Pre-Fab
Port as big as Dover**
*Composite aerial photograph
showing the extent and
complexity of the
British Mulberry Harbour
at Arromanches.*

Key to photograph
1 *Bombardons
(not shown on photograph)*
2 *Phœnix caissons*
3 *Entrance channel*
4 *Sheltered water*
5 *Scuttled ships*
6 *Quays*
7 *Pier roadways*
8 *Beach*

This Miraculous Port

Prime Minister Churchill visited the harbour at Arromanches on 23 July. Returning to England he gave his personal view of its significance to Captain Harold Hickling, the Naval officer in charge of the British Mulberry:

> This miraculous port has played, and will continue to play, a most important part in the liberation of Europe. [16]

Hickling himself later wrote in his report that 'There is no escaping the basic facts that the operation was successful'. No prudent commander could have launched Operation Overlord 'without the assurance that his minimum maintenance requirements could be landed unimpeded by the vagaries of the Channel weather'. [17]

For Commander Lochner and one of his senior colleagues in the Lilo team, an inspection soon after D-Day brought clear evidence that all their efforts had met with success. Crossing to France they then took a rowing boat to examine how the Bombardons were working. A considerable wind was blowing, but on their lee side the sea was quite calm with waves of no more than eighteen inches. Spray rising as high as twenty feet above the Bombardons gave proof that they were well absorbing the force of the waves rolling in from the open sea.

Few historians today would argue with Churchill or Hickling in their assessment of the contribution of the artificial harbours to the allied invasion of Europe. It was a gigantic undertaking and one of the most imaginative engineering projects of World War Two. If the importance of the Mulberry project cannot be over-estimated, then neither can the personal contribution of Robert Lochner.

In March 1948 his role in originating and developing the floating outer breakwater was examined by the Royal Commission on Awards to Inventors. They heard that he was not only the inspiration

60 **Arromanches**
Supplies come ashore.

61 **Arromanches**
Jeeps come ashore.

behind the idea, but also the driving force behind the project from start to finish. A grant of an ex-gratia payment of £1,000 was seen by many at the time as inappropriate and inadequate recognition for one who contributed so much to the Normandy bridgehead and so to the success of the allied invasion. He was awarded the MBE. [18]

CHAPTER 7

DESTINATION - THE FAR SHORE

Dance before Battle

On 26 May 1944 General Eisenhower lunched with the King and Queen at Buckingham Palace. That evening he ordered that the Halcyon Plus 4 message, previously sent to Washington, should be repeated to all subordinate commands in the United Kingdom, sounding the alert that D-Day would be 5 June.

As the message sped to headquarters throughout the country, a dance was being held in the drill hall at Worthing by the Scots Greys and the Gordon Highlanders, two regiments whose combined charge at the Battle of Waterloo had been commemorated by Lady Butler's well known painting. Their dance on this occasion cannot fail to arouse faint echoes of the Duchess of Richmond's famous ball on the eve of Waterloo.

62 **Monty in Worthing**
Montgomery leaves the Town Hall after meeting the Mayor.

For troops in Petworth Park and the many other Concentration and Marshalling Areas earmarked to be in the forefront of the coming assault, 0100 Hours on 26 May marked the start of X-Day. This was the day on which their camps were sealed and troops 'vanished' from the outside world until the dawn of D-Day.

General Sir Bernard Montgomery, Commander-in-Chief, Land Forces, visits the 4th Armoured Brigade at their invasion HQ at Worthing, 25 May 1944.

63 **Meeting the Troops**
His flamboyance, self-assurance and dynamic personality made him a popular military leader.

DESTINATION - THE FAR SHORE

A Vanishing Army

The main purpose of the sealing of these camps was to allow for briefing of the assault troops on their D-Day roles, keeping the risk of any security leaks to a minimum.

All these troops were now confined to camp. Now only a few troops of outside army units and the few civilians issued with special passes were given entry. The most important principle of the operation was that no person who had been briefed should be allowed to come into contact with any others who had not been so briefed. To help this distinction soldiers yet to be given classified information were ordered to wear a distinguishing mark on their left shoulder strap. All public houses, clubs, cafés, shops, cinemas and other places of entertainment were put out of bounds. Outgoing telephone calls and telegrams were banned and the posting of mail suspended until after D-Day. Troops temporarily leaving camps on duty, or in transit to Marshalling Areas, were forbidden to speak to civilians. Any of those who became ill or were injured in accidents had to be taken to specially isolated hospitals.

64 **Careless Talk Costs Lives**
Security intensifies
as D-Day approaches.

Both camps 1 and 2 in Petworth Park had been sealed on 26 May. Intensive briefing of the 27th Armoured Brigade now started. Some huts were turned into intelligence centres to which came a constant flow of information about enemy beach defences, about strong points that would have to be attacked, and the characteristics and weapons of enemy forces.

65 **Music While You Work!**
In Petworth Park the band
of 13/18th Royal Hussars
plays to tank crews busy
stowing ammunition and stores
in readiness for the move to
their Marshalling Area
at Waterlooville,
30 May 1944.

DESTINATION - THE FAR SHORE

Information now given to the troops included highly detailed diagrams and relief models of the enemy fortifications. Large numbers of aerial photographs gave close detail of the exact spots in which they would land, but the precise identification of the landing beaches was still not revealed. Real names of towns, villages and other topographical features they now studied on maps were only known by code-names. Not until the very last minute was their exact destination revealed. It continued to be known as `The Far Shore', a phrase familiar to the troops in all their training.

Whitsun had now come. Right up to the end of May the fine weather persisted on both sides of the Channel.

On 28 May Admiral Friedrich Ruge, naval adviser to Rommel, summed up the mood of the day in his diary: `Beautiful weather. General astonishment and joy that the enemy did not take advantage of it. We played tennis and table tennis.' [1]

Even as these words were being written the roads of Sussex were thronged with long columns of vehicles. They bore the sea horse badge of the 27th Armoured Brigade, the red dagger of the Commandos, the triangle of the 3rd Division, the anchor of the Beach Groups, the crusader crosses of the 21st Army Group and 2nd Army and the spearhead and boar rampant signs of the 1st and 30th Corps. The movement of assault forces from Concentration to Marshalling Areas was now entering its final stage.

British 30th Corps

In towns such as Worthing where troops and their vehicles had become such familiar sights, residents now faced strangely empty streets and green spaces. Keith Downer was a seventeen year old living in Worthing as D-Day approached:

> The last few days before 6 June 1944 endless convoys of troops and tanks passed through the town. When the Royal Scots Greys passed with their Sherman tanks, we were surprised to see two local lads, Bob and Frank Collins from King Street, among the troops as they made a brief stop outside the old Boys' High School in Broadwater, and we managed to exchange a brief conversation. Where for weeks before the Brighton Road, Broadwater, Goring and Findon areas had been packed with vehicles and troops, all was suddenly empty. [2]

Armoured divisions left a strong impression on local residents as they made their cumbersome way to the Marshalling and Assembly Areas. Convoys left their mark on road surfaces and on the corners of buildings. Leslie Howell remembers the roads suffering in Midhurst:

> With the approach of D-Day....the movement of vehicles of all sorts increased.
> Low flying aircraft sported the black-and-white invasion stripes and the white star appeared on less glamorous machines. Probably the highlight for Midhurst at this time was the passing through of an armoured division on their way to their assembly point. They were routed via North Street, Knockhundred Row, West Street and Petersfield Road. With the narrow roads, the tanks could only follow one line and with the swivel action of their tracks were soon through the metalling of the road surface on the corners.
> So after each tank went by a gang of council workmen were there to shovel back into the hole what the tank had turned out. [3]

As the last of the convoys wound their way towards the Portsmouth area, or towards Shoreham and Newhaven, the first signs appeared that the long spell of fine spring weather was about to end.

First light on 1 June found the day dull and cloudy. The SHAEF meteorological team at Southwick House, near Portsmouth - now Eisenhower's Advanced Headquarters - found that an unusual weather pattern was starting to develop over the Atlantic. Early in the day the head of the team, Group Captain James Stagg, was still fairly optimistic about the prospects for 5 June. By evening he was having increased doubts, and to make matters worse, SHAEF and Admiralty experts were divided about the probable outlook. When he admitted his own doubts, a somewhat rattled senior American staff officer exclaimed 'For heaven's sake, Stagg, get it sorted out by tomorrow morning before you come to the Supreme Commander's conference. General Eisenhower is a very worried man.'[4]

66 **Petworth Convoy**

A special Armoured Recovery Vehicle Tank - a modified Sherman - passing a line of parked Sherman tanks during the move of the 27th Armoured Brigade from Petworth.

67 **God Speed!**

A young lady offers milk and good wishes to a Sherman tank crew of the 13/18th Royal Hussars. Their journey from Petworth took them first to Waterlooville and then to Gosport for embarkation.

DESTINATION - THE FAR SHORE

The Ports

Although the majority of the assault forces concentrated in West Sussex were to embark from the Portsmouth area, some did so through either Shoreham or Newhaven.

Troops embarking from these two ports first passed through J Marshalling Area extending from beyond Seaford in the east to Portslade, just outside Brighton, in the west. Its northern border reached to Haywards Heath. Area headquarters was at Lewes and it controlled ten principal Marshalling Camps. Some of these were at Firle Park near Lewes, Stanmer Park near Brighton, Borde Hill near Haywards Heath and Wykehurst Park at Bolney. The camps had a combined capacity for 15,000 men and 2,380 vehicles at any one time.

68 **Wykehurst Park**
Site of one of the Marshalling Camps in J Area for troops embarking from Shoreham and Newhaven.

It is an indication of the vast resources needed to mount Operation Overlord that the staffing and maintenance of these camps, and the provision of what were known as 'hotel services', employed personnel of two infantry battalions, an artillery regiment and most of an armoured regiment not immediately involved in the invasion. Other units were needed to provide construction work and transport services.

From the Marshalling Camps, troops on their way to embarkation moved first to Assembly Areas close to the ports. Here commanders received final instructions about how units should be split for embarkation in the different crafts. When the units had been divided into shipping loads they then moved into a Transit Area to wait embarkation.

As the initial assault forces and then the D-Day follow-up forces moved from Concentration Areas to Marshalling Areas, formations and units scheduled to move to France at a later date were on the move all over the country to fill the vacancies in the Concentration Areas. There they waited, to follow on through the same process in an almost continuous stream.

Assault forces embarking at Newhaven included some units of the 3rd Infantry Division and the first line transport of the 27th Armoured Brigade. This last unit carried vital supplies of ammunition and other essentials. Immediately following D-Day the nine berths of the port saw a constant stream of follow-up forces of many roles and size, including the 15th Scottish Division and the Guards Armoured Division. Newhaven served as a major supply port for British forces on the continent extending well into the following winter. The port also served as a major route for incoming German prisoners-of-war on their way to British prison camps.

Littlehampton made a vital contribution to D-Day operations and the Normandy campaign as an ammunition supply port. Early in May, nine barges arrived in the harbour to be loaded with some 2,700 tons of ammunition, and then before D-Day nine small ships were similarly loaded. Their job was to re-supply the assault forces as quickly as possible after the first landings. Subsequently an ammunition ship sailed from Littlehampton every day. By the end of August approximately 18,000 tons had reached France from the little port. [5]

DESTINATION - THE FAR SHORE

Connie Westerdick served in the WRNS at Littlehampton during the build-up to D-Day and remembers that barges, each said to be loaded with 400 tons of ammunition, were tied up to the banks of the Arun 'for miles inland'. They were towed down river and out to sea after D-Day. One major incident was averted when there was a near miss by a Dutch coaster entering port against orders, much to the consternation of the harbour master.

Her work was connected with Defensively Equipped Merchant Ships which used Littlehampton and were to play a crucial part in the D-Day operations. She drove a 15 cwt. truck, collecting boxes of ammunition and parts of Lewis and Oerlikon guns from the public air raid shelters by the Swing Bridge, delivering them to the old lifeboat house near Butlin's amusement park on the seafront where they were unloaded by two sailors. Her truck journeys through the centre of Littlehampton with their vital loads for the small ships were supervised by a marine sergeant in peacetime uniform.

The Littlehampton quaysides were busy handling the military supplies, and country roads outside the town were lined with corrugated iron shelters packed with stores. In the shipyard a motor torpedo boat was under construction. Three 'fast and business-like' RAF launches were either tied up in the harbour or seen on most days 'heading out to sea behind an impressive bow wave'.

69 **Littlehampton**
Landing craft berthed on the banks of the River Arun in readiness for D-Day. There were landing craft construction sites at Bosham and Itchenor.

Miss Westerdick recalls that security surrounding the work of the port was extremely tight during the final stages of the build-up:

> Civilian telephone calls out of the area were not permitted for those few weeks.
> There was no long distance dialling then, so monitoring was strict. I could not ring my
> worried parents and the pillar boxes were all sealed, so that I had to post my letters home
> through the Fleet Mail Office, whose official stamp on the envelopes convinced Mother
> that I was already at sea.[6]

Invasion Postponed

The SHAEF Supreme Commander's conference on the morning of 2 June took place in the library of Southwick House, now operational headquarters. General Eisenhower, General Montgomery - whose A Mess was at nearby Broomfield House[7] - and senior air and naval officers sat on sofas and chairs in an informal ring.

DESTINATION - THE FAR SHORE

As the tall figure of the RAF's Chief Meteorological Officer, Group Captain Stagg, left the room after giving his forecast, one British Admiral remarked: 'Six feet two of Stagg, and six feet one of gloom'. [8]

During the next forty-eight hours the Group Captain's fears that the weather was starting to turn 'untrustworthy' were justified in full measure as one depression after another started to fill the North Atlantic. 'The weather in this country is practically unpredictable' wrote General Eisenhower in a memorandum containing a hint of exasperation. [9] He now gave orders that he wanted weather forecasts twice a day.

*70 **Embarkation***
US troops carrying
full battle equipment
crowd aboard a landing craft.

Within the next twenty-four hours weather patterns started to develop in such an erratic and unusual manner that it was only possible to give forecasts of any accuracy for six to twelve hours ahead, not the usual forty-eight hours. Two weather stations were producing contrary forecasts.

That evening Eisenhower and Montgomery dined together at Broomfield House and then went to another conference at Southwick. The experts still had no very clear idea about weather prospects for 5 June, but it was decided that the existing plan should go ahead subject to review at a further conference the next evening.

By now assault troops were boarding their various craft at all the Overlord embarkation ports. The 13/18th Hussars moved out of the Marshalling Camp at Waterlooville near Portsmouth, where it had concentrated after its departure from Petworth two days before, and loaded its DD and other tanks onto their allotted landing craft. In the Marshalling Areas many troops had now been issued with French money and a little booklet informing them they were going to France as part of a 'new British Expeditionary Force'. But there was still no mention of the word 'Normandy'.

*71 **Well Equipped***
Before leaving England
invasion troops were issued
with a few francs, a guide book
on France and basic rations,
including cigarettes.

DESTINATION - THE FAR SHORE

Jim Wheeler, serving with 11 Light Field Ambulance, part of the 27th Armoured Brigade, remembers that there was now some time for relaxation in the Marshalling and Assembly Areas. The film *Cassablanca* was shown night and day in a large marquee in his camp at Rowlands Castle. By D-Day he knew the film word for word. [10]

Part of the 2nd Battalion of The East Yorkshire Regiment which was in the 3rd Division's 8th Brigade - due to take the lead in the attack on Sword Beach - had been transferred from its Marshalling Camp at Cowplain in Hampshire, to another away in East Sussex at Firle Park, near Lewes. One soldier recalls men whiling away the time waiting for the order to embark by exchanging 'the invasion money' for ordinary cash 'mainly for gambling, and small fortunes were won and lost in quick time'. [11]

When the commanders met again at Southwick House on Saturday evening on 3 June the weather forecasts had become sharply more discouraging. Three large depressions were bringing bad weather into the Channel. Over the three days chosen to launch the assault it was likely that the Channel would be affected by high winds and thick cloud. The gathering decided to assemble again for a final decision about a possible postponement at 4.30 the following morning.

Once more assembled in the library at that early hour, those present knew there could be no further delay. Admiral Sir Bertram Ramsay, Commander-in-Chief, Allied Naval Forces, reminded them that the decision must be made within thirty minutes if the sailing of the main assault force was to be halted, and if convoys carrying American troops from West Country ports already on their way were to be turned round. After Group Captain Stagg had been unable to report any improvement on the weather forecast he had given the previous evening, and after a short discussion, Eisenhower gave the order for the assault to be postponed by one day. By 11 that morning the Admiralty was issuing gale warnings for the Channel. A rapidly rising wind whistling through the trees around Southwick House convinced all that had the invasion gone ahead a major disaster might well have resulted.

72 **Bound for Normandy**
US troops 'somewhere in Southern England' marching to their embarkation port.

Marching down the road from Firle to their waiting landing craft at Newhaven, the 2nd East Yorks had been stopped in their tracks and returned to camp. Most of the invasion convoys at sea returned to port without difficulty. Clifford Robinson - now Chairman of West Sussex County Council - served with the 10th Beach Signals Section, attached to the 185th Brigade, 3rd Infantry Division. He had embarked from Shoreham on an LCT (Landing Craft, Tank) and well remembers turning back for Newhaven in the middle of a storm on receiving the postponement order. After a brief respite at their embarkation base in Stanmer Park his unit returned to Newhaven under close escort. Finally sailing on the night of 5 June, and landing at Hermanville-sur-Mer, the 10th Beach Signals provided vital communication links for the invasion forces on Sword Beach. [12]

DESTINATION - THE FAR SHORE

The decision to postpone was not immediately heeded by one large American convoy sailing from the West Country. It was apparently glimpsed by some pilots from Ford as it continued to plough steadily towards the French coast for some five hours after the decision had been made. Ignoring all wireless signals it was eventually persuaded to return only when a message was dropped onto the deck of its leading ship by a British aircraft.

On board one of the tank landing craft assigned to the 27th Armoured Brigade sheltering in the Solent, the chaplain of the 13/18th Hussars, the Reverend Victor Leach, took advantage of the postponement to hold a Sunday morning service. Of this he afterwards wrote:

> I think everyone attended. Previously it was difficult to get anyone to a service. The only thing I remember about the service was that we sang the hymn 'Eternal Father, strong to save'. Never before or since have I heard the refrain sung so feelingly 'O hear us when we cry to Thee, For those in peril on the sea'. The LCT that was to the lee of ours signalled asking me to conduct a service on that landing craft. The midshipman came across in a dinghy and I duly held a second service. [13]

The problems confronting the senior allied commanders if weather forecasts for 6 June produced no signs of improvement were now truly forbidding. Some of the assault troops had already been confined in cramped quarters aboard their vessels for some seventy-two hours. Some in more exposed anchorages, or in the convoys that had been recalled, were suffering badly from seasickness. Clearly they could not be kept aboard for another fortnight until the middle of June when the conditions for a dawn landing would again be right. Yet to return so many thousands of men who had already been briefed to their Marshalling or Concentration Areas would obviously present the most appalling security risks. The strain on morale of yet another period of waiting might become unbearable. The only other possible solution might be to attempt a landing not at dawn but under conditions of full daylight when tides were right on 8 or 9 June. But this would deprive the invasion fleet of the cover of darkness as it approached the shore.

It is not surprising that to some who observed General Eisenhower that Sunday he appeared at times to be 'bowed down with worry....as though each of the four stars on either shoulder weighed a ton'. In the afternoon he could occasionally be seen coming to the door of the trailer in which he worked in the grounds of Southwick House. He would glance up at the cloud-covered sky, or walk up and down outside the trailer, chain smoking, 'kicking at the cinders on the little pathway - a tall figure, shoulders slightly hunched, hands rammed deep into his pockets'.

On one occasion he spotted an American war correspondent he knew and asked him to come for a walk. The correspondent later said that it was a very silent walk. The General hardly spoke: 'Ike seemed completely preoccupied with his own thoughts, completely immersed in all his problems..... It was almost as though he had forgotten I was with him.' [14]

Grey Suede Shoes

Field Marshal Rommel was well known by his staff as an early riser. On Sunday 4 June he had a particular reason for being so, a reason nothing to do with any sudden warning of an imminent allied landing. Messages and reports he had recently received gave no cause for fearing that such an onslaught was at hand. [15] Early that morning the German naval command in Cherbourg had ruled out any chance of immediate attack because of the weather.

It seems that the German commander had few qualms about making an early start for the long drive back to Berlin. There he intended to spend a day or two at home to celebrate the fiftieth birthday of his wife, Lucie-Maria, which fell ironically on Tuesday 6 June. He wished to deliver her birthday present, a pair of grey suede shoes he had ordered in Paris. Afterwards he would visit Hitler in an attempt to secure the Fuhrer's consent to move two Panzer divisions nearer the French Channel coast so they would be better placed to engage in the immediate counter-attack against any allied landing. A counter-attack he believed essential if the German Army in France was not to face defeat.

Illness had resulted in Rommel's absence from his post at the head of the Afrika Korps at the onset of the Battle of El Alamein in 1942. Now fate was to decree that when his old foe Montgomery struck yet again, Rommel would be absent from his headquarters once more, this time for fourteen out of the first twenty-four hours of the fighting, a twenty-four hours he himself had forecast would be decisive.

Historic Decision

'Survey urgently needed of harbour moorings on the entire English south coast by air reconnaissance' read one paragraph of Rommel's weekly situation report on the morning of Monday 5 June. [16]

It was a need that was never met. Weather conditions that day ensured that the only reconnaissance flight the Luftwaffe could make was an unproductive one off the Dutch coast.

Whilst Rommel was back in Germany, yet another meeting was being held in the library at Southwick House. It was probably one of the most historic conferences in the history of the war. General Montgomery afterwards wrote of it:

> We met at 4 a.m. A heavy storm was blowing in the Channel and it was clear that if we had persisted with the original D-Day of the 5th June, we might have had a disaster.

> But the Met. reports indicated a slackening of the storm, and a period of reasonable weather on the 6th June. Indeed, the experts predicted reasonable weather for some days after the 6th June before the next period of unsettled weather arrived.

> On that Eisenhower decided to go. We were all glad. This conference did not last more than 15 minutes. Eisenhower was in good form and made his decision quickly. [17]

That evening B Watch WAAF plotters coming on duty in the Operations Room in Chichester's Bishop Otter College - presided over as usual by Squadron Leader Lord Dunkley accompanied as always by his dachshund - were quickly struck by the fact that the many ship symbols on the plotting table were all pointing away from the English coast. So they could not be coastal convoys. They must be the start of the long-awaited allied invasion. [18]

Out in the countryside near Findon soldiers of the 2nd Battalion Gordon Highlanders were exercising on a fine late spring night. They looked up to see some 300 aircraft towing gliders in a two-hour long procession outlined against the full moon. These same aircraft returned before very long without their gliders. D-Day had come at last.

The sleep of few in West Sussex that night remained unbroken by the steady drone of aircraft overhead.

21 ARMY GROUP

PERSONAL MESSAGE
FROM THE C-IN-C

(To be read out to all Troops)

1. The time has come to deal the enemy a terrific blow in Western Europe.
   The blow will be struck by the combined sea, land, and air forces of the Allies—together constituting one great Allied team, under the supreme command of General Eisenhower.

2. On the eve of this great adventure I send my best wishes to every soldier in the Allied team.
   To us is given the honour of striking a blow for freedom which will live in history; and in the better days that lie ahead men will speak with pride of our doings. We have a great and a righteous cause.
   Let us pray that "The Lord Mighty in Battle" will go forth with our armies, and that His special providence will aid us in the struggle.

3. I want every soldier to know that I have complete confidence in the successful outcome of the operations that we are now about to begin.
   With stout hearts, and with enthusiasm for the contest, let us go forward to victory.

4. And, as we enter the battle, let us recall the words of a famous soldier spoken many years ago:—

   > "He either fears his fate too much,
   > Or his deserts are small,
   > Who dare not put it to the touch,
   > To win or lose it all."

5. Good luck to each one of you. And good hunting on the mainland of Europe.

B. L. Montgomery

General,
C.-in-C.,
21 Army Group.

73 **Eve of Invasion Message,
5 June 1944**

CHAPTER 8

THE LONGEST DAY

In the days leading up to 6 June local people in West Sussex had become aware of the growing tension as preparations for invasion reached their inevitable climax. The assembling of the Mulberry components, landing craft in harbours, increased aerial activity, convoys of armoured vehicles as well as huge troop movements all gave rise to the feeling that the day was near at hand.

Winifred Langer, living in the village of Sidlesham on the Manhood peninsula near Chichester, recalls that a lone German plane unwittingly stumbled on last minute activities in the Selsey area:

> As D-Day approached, every wayside tree sheltered a gun or truck; a Mulberry Harbour appeared near the entrance to Pagham harbour. Sighted by a solitary German plane, an air raid followed and all the guns ready for D-Day blazed forth - the noisiest night locally! Shortly, at night with pinpoint lights and nose to tail, the soldiers who had been gathered locally, together with all their equipment, quietly departed. Local people lined the road; all the canteen chocolate and cigarettes were pressed into the men's hands and we wished them God Speed.[1]

The departure of the assault troops and their white-starred invasion vehicles presented an exciting spectacle for school children lucky enough to witness the scene. Maurice Wilson-Voke was a pupil at the Lancastrian Boys' School in Orchard Street, Chichester. He remembers that as the D-Day troops passed by all the boys risked the wrath of their headmaster to get a good view:

> I attended school during the day time and there was a great deal of heavy military traffic - lorries, tanks and many bren gun carriers. In the front of the school there were lawns. If you were caught walking on them you got 'six of the best'. As they came by we all rushed over the lawns to the iron railings on Orchard Street to cheer the soldiers on the tanks and lorries. They cheered and waved back. When the bell went after lunch the teachers were reluctant to blow their whistles to get us back in.[2]

74 **The Daily Business**
War and peace in a Southern English town as troops and civilians await D-Day.

THE LONGEST DAY

Twenty miles away in Worthing Lois Jordan was at church with her mother - at Christ Church - the day before invasion. She recalls the service being interrupted by the commanding officer of a unit attending church parade:

> The commanding officer marched right up just as the sermon was starting and said all the men must leave....the vicar said, 'Could you give me just one minute to talk to the men', and it was granted, just to give them a bit of encouragement. It was really very beautiful. The next day we heard France had been invaded. After that we didn't have any soldiers in the town.[3]

D-Day Home Front

For officers manning the Royal Observer Corps post near Telegraph Hill, high on the South Downs at Compton - between Chichester and Petersfield - the evening of Monday 5 June had been busy. Aerial activity then built-up from midnight, with bombers overhead making for France. Then at 2.30 the following morning came the first indication of the airborne invasion with the reporting of glider-towing aircraft going over. Their log records 167 separate entries on D-Day itself. Some were sightings of fifty or more planes at once and include a galaxy of allied aircraft: Dakotas, Fortresses, Lancasters, Liberators, Lightnings, Marauders, Mosquitos, Mustangs, Spitfires, Thunderbolts and Typhoons.[4]

6th Airborne Division

Bognor, Littlehampton and Worthing were directly under the flight paths of the 6th Airborne Division as it headed for Normandy. Throughout the long night of 5/6 June the drone of aircraft overhead gave clear signs that the long-awaited invasion had at last begun. Glider-towing tugs and paratrooper transporters from airfields in Oxfordshire, Berkshire, Wiltshire and Dorset, converged on these three West Sussex rendezvous points before the Channel crossing, guided by specially-installed Eureka navigation beacons and flashing lights on the coastline. Return flights for all aircraft were to be over Littlehampton at 3,000 feet. To identify them to allied sea, air and ground forces all aircraft were marked with three white and two black stripes on the wings and fuselage.[5]

Keith Downer of Worthing remembers the night vividly and that not all the gliders succeeded in their mission:

> That night....I went to sleep, but the noise was continuous the whole night with the passing overhead of hundreds of bombers and Dakota transport aircraft, conveying the men of the 6th Airborne Division as they passed over Worthing on their way to invade France. It went

75 **Air Assault**
Airborne divisions were the first to set foot in occupied Europe on D-Day. Paratroopers went in first, followed by units landing in gliders. Here the aircraft reach the Normandy coastline as the invasion fleet below approaches the beaches.

on and on for hour after hour, until one began to think the whole allied army was being taken across in one night. In the morning we learned that the British and American armies had landed and were doing well. But meanwhile, in Worthing, one of the huge Horsa gliders, full of troops, had broken away from its tow plane and landed safely on the Selden lawns, Brighton Road, whilst another had landed on the Downs at Sompting close to Pullen Berry Nursery. Both of these aircraft being later collected by the military.[6]

The official confirmation that the invasion was under way came in a morning wireless bulletin and was sufficient to persuade this eager seventeen year old that duty called:

> I rushed home and changed into my Home Guard uniform and sat with my rifle awaiting a hostile retaliation landing of German troops to disrupt the landings. But nothing happened and for me it became an anti-climax that sank into despair, and feeling of being 'there', but not part of it.[7]

Joan Strange was also in Worthing throughout the war years where she kept a daily diary of her experiences. She served as a volunteer receiving and passing on telephone messages at the ARP Report Centre in the Town Hall. Despite the importance of this particular Tuesday she passed a relatively quiet time:

> June 6th
> Today has proved to be D-Day. We awoke at 5 a.m. to hear peculiar sounding planes flying over - gliders apparently. On the 8 a.m. news it was reported that the Germans had broadcast that we'd dropped paratroops in France. By midday everyone seemed to know *it* had happened at last. We'd had large convoys of troops in all sorts of vehicles passing through Worthing for the last two days and planes had been very active. We listened in at the Report Centre and heard that 4,000 ships had taken part and many thousands of small ones. Normandy was the chosen spot and Mr. Churchill made a statement that the first landings had been successful. He wanted to go himself but was dissuaded. Funnily enough it's been quieter in the air over here today and there was 'nothing to report' on duty at the Report Centre.[8]

Living in nearby Sompting at this time was Peter Driscoll, a teenager evacuated from London at the beginning of the war with his two younger brothers. Later, during the Blitz, they were joined by their mother and two sisters. Very early on D-Day morning their sleep had been disturbed by the sound of the airborne armada overhead. Emerging in the light of day, the children found that the friendly soldiers who had given them cap badges and shoulder flashes had now left, their heavily

76 **Glider Attack**
The sleep of few people in West Sussex was undisturbed on the night of 5/6 June as aircraft of the 6th Airborne Division flew overhead en route to Normandy. Here Halifaxes and Hamilcar Gliders of the 6th Division fly over the landing beaches.

armoured vehicles and bren gun carriers covered in camouflage-netting now gone from the roadsides:

> On the early morning of 6 June the whole family was awakened by the heavy drone of aircraft heading across the Channel. There were fighters, bombers and Dakotas towing gliders filled with airborne troops. They seemed to be never ending. Later that morning came the allied broadcast that troops had invaded the north coast of France and had gained a foothold. We noticed that all the troops and armoured vehicles had gone overnight, bringing to mind the old saying 'here today and gone tomorrow', although of course there was still the odd convoy of supply and armoured vehicles heading for the docks.[9]

At Sidlesham Winifred Langer clearly remembers hearing the Dakotas passing over with their gliders in tow:

> As dawn broke on D-Day we heard the drone of planes with gliders attached, rank on rank, stretching away to Littlehampton. On the ground everyone went to their action post and the sound of gunfire towards the French coast was heard. We did not need the news by radio at 8 a.m. to tell us that the invasion of the French coast had begun.[10]

The drama overhead that night clearly indicated what must be happening on the far coast, but as listeners anxiously clustered round their wireless sets they had to wait until 9.30 in the morning for the official confirmation that the invasion had started. The confirmation came with the issue of the first, and somewhat vaguely worded, SHAEF communiqué. There was little more precise information for the rest of the day. This was in part because of the security blanket, but also because for some twelve hours allied headquarters in England - and even some HQ ships in the Channel - were woefully short of factual information. At the time this first communiqué was issued the only hard news received by Eisenhower and Montgomery was based on fragmentary reports indicating that the airborne landings had been successful. Until he left for Normandy that evening, Montgomery waited in the garden at Broomfield House. Eisenhower, drinking endless cups of coffee, waited for more news in his trailer at Southwick.

77 **First News**
First official confirmation of the allied invasion came in early morning wireless bulletins. The evening newspapers of 6 June give the first detailed reports of what was happening.

This initial lack of information was caused partly by technical communication problems, and partly by a flood of incoming messages to SHAEF headquarters from the public, politicians and others. The switchboards were jammed, delaying the transcription of operational radio messages.

The growing intensity of the fighting across the Channel was clear to people living in the vicinity of the South Coast airfields as wave upon wave of fighters were scrambled throughout the day. As they watched the planes come and go that morning they could not have known that for some six hours the fate of Operation Overlord hung in the balance as disaster - ultimately overcome - threatened to overwhelm the American assault on Omaha Beach.

TUESDAY, JUNE 6, 1944

Evening Standard

37,357   BLACK-OUT 10 57 pm to 5.0 am   MOON Rises 9.50 pm; Sets 6 29 am   ONE PENNY

FINAL NIGHT EXTRA

Churchill Announces Successful Massed Air Landings Behind Enemy in France

4000 SHIPS, THOUSANDS OF SMALLER VESSELS

"So Far All Goes to Plan"— 11,000 First Line Airplanes

An immense armada of more than 4000 ships, with several thousand smaller craft, has crossed the Channel, said Mr. Churchill to-day, announcing the invasion.

"MASSED AIRBORNE LANDINGS HAVE BEEN SUCCESSFULLY EFFECTED BEHIND THE ENEMY'S LINES," HE SAID.

MR. CHURCHILL DESCRIBED THE LANDINGS AS THE "FIRST OF A SERIES IN FORCE ON THE EUROPEAN CONTINENT."

"The landings on the beaches are proceeding at various points at the present time. The fire of the shore batteries has been largely quelled, said Mr. Churchill.

"The obstacles which were constructed in the sea have not proved so difficult as was apprehended.

"The Anglo-American Allies are sustained by about 11,000 first line aircraft, which can be drawn upon as may be needed for the purposes of the battle.

No. 1

At 9.30 a.m. to-day the following communiqué was issued from General Eisenhower's Supreme Headquarters:

"Under the command of General Eisenhower, Allied naval forces, supported by strong air forces, began landing Allied armies this morning on the Northern coast of France."

The statement was marked "Communiqué No. 1." At the same time it was revealed that General Montgomery is in command of the Army Group carrying out the assault. This Army Group includes British, Canadian and U.S. forces.

The King on the Radio To-night

It was officially announced from Buckingham Palace to-day that the King will broadcast at 9 o'clock to-night.

HITLER IN COMMAND

Hitler is taking personal command of all the anti-invasion operations, according to news reaching London from underground sources.

His four marshals are Rundstedt, titular commander-in-chief; Rommel, Inspector-General; Sperrle, in charge of air forces; and Blaskowitz, acting deputy to Rommel.

"I cannot, of course, commit myself to any particular details, as reports are coming in in rapid succession. So far, the commanders who are engaged report that everything is proceeding according to plan—and what a plan!

"This vast operation is undoubtedly the most complicated and difficult that has ever occurred.

SURPRISE

"There are already hopes that actual tactical surprise has been attained," said the Premier, "and we hope to furnish the enemy with a succession of surprises during the course of the fighting.

"The battle which is now beginning will grow constantly in scale and in intensity for many weeks to come, and I shall not attempt to speculate upon its course.

"Complete unity prevails throughout the Allied Armies. (Cheers.)

"There is a brotherhood in arms between us and our friends in the United States.

"There is complete confidence in the Supreme Commander, General Eisenhower, and in his lieutenants, and also in the Commander of the Expeditionary Force, General Montgomery.

"The ardour and spirit of the troops as I saw them myself embarking in these last few days was splendid.

"Nothing that equipment, science and forethought can do has been neglected, and the whole process of opening this great new front will be pursued with the utmost resolution both by the commanders and by the US and British Governments whom they serve.

WHAT A PLAN!

Replying to Mr. Greenwood Mr. Churchill said that certainly in the early part of the battle he

(Continued on Back Page, Col. Four)

'LANDINGS ON JERSEY, GUERNSEY'

German Overseas News Agency said this afternoon that landings have been made on the Channel Islands —Jersey and Guernsey—by Allied parachute troops.

Quoting the German High Command spokesman, the agency said: "Early to-day Allied airborne formations landed on Guernsey and Jersey.

"They were at once engaged in extremely costly battles."

Thousands Of Fighters Strafe The Nazi Guns

Since the invasion began, Allied fighter-bombers have been dive-bombing, glide-bombing and strafing German defences and communications.

They fly literally into the mouths of guns and dive within feet of the spans which hold bridges together.

A gun is silenced, a truck carrying ammunition for a company of German soldiers is blown up, a bridge is shattered making German supply convoys detour 20 or 30 miles, a gun crew is wiped out—multiplied by thousands, the fighter-bomber attacks will help the surface forces in 1000 ways, and will have an enormous effect on the battles below.

Bomber Command last night made their heaviest attack to date on the German batteries along the French coast.

In all, Bomber Command despatched more than 1300 aircraft.

SHELLED BY 640 GUNS

The Supreme Headquarters of the Allied Expeditionary Force state that over 640 naval guns, from 16in. to 4in., are bombarding the beaches and enemy strong points in support of the armies.

About 200 Allied minesweepers, with 10,000 officers and men, are engaged in the operations.

The weight of minesweeping material used amounts to 2800 tons, and the amount of sweep wire in use would reach almost exactly from London to the Isle of Wight.

The Press Association learns that enemy destroyers and E-boats are reported coming into the operational area.

'Tanks Ashore on Normandy Coast'

—SAYS BERLIN

The Allies have established beach-heads in Northern France and are driving inland, according to pilots who have flown over the battle.

This afternoon the Germans announced that landings were continuing in the Seine Bay—the stretch of the Normandy coast between the two ports of Cherbourg and Le Havre.

They reported parachute landings on Guernsey and Jersey, the two principal Channel Islands, and said that Allied troops were ashore at these points on the coast of Normandy:

ST. VAAST LE HOUGE (on the Cherbourg Peninsula): "Mass landing" supported by considerable naval forces, while strong American airborne forces jumped near Barfleur, a few miles to the north.

OUISTREHAM (at the mouth of the River Orne): "Landing barges under strong air umbrella are making landings," said the Germans.

Earlier the Germans had mentioned that Caen, a few miles inland up the Orne was "the first local point," where sharp fighting was taking place. The Germans also reported fighting 10 miles inland.

ARROMANCHES (in the middle of the Seine Bay): Tanks have been landed there says Berlin.

ST. MARCOUF ISLANDS (just off the coast south of Cherbourg): "New landings made before noon particularly in this area."

VIRE ESTUARY

Another focal point mentioned by the Germans was the estuary of the Vire, another river running north into the Seine Bay.

Parachute landings were reported in several areas before daybreak.

(Continued on Back Page, Col. 7)

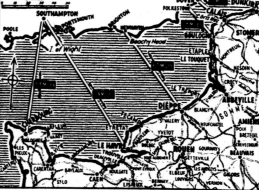

Stories of The Men Who Watched

Here are the stories told by men who watched the landings.

Fighter pilots returning from over the landing areas report that Allied infantry scrambled ashore at 7 a.m. in two areas of the French coast, apparently without heavy opposition, says Robert Richards, British United Press war correspondent at a U.S. Fighter Base.

One of the pilots, an American Colonel, William Curry, told me:

"I saw the first troops wading ashore about 7 a.m., from light landing craft. From the height at which I was flying they did not appear to be meeting heavy opposition and were covered by extensive and heavy naval bombardment from our warships.

"Flying Fortresses were also bombing the beach which appeared to be marshy instead of sandy. Major John Locke, of Texas, who led a squadron of Thunderbolts, said:

"I have never seen so many ships in all my life. Flying over the harbour at one port I counted great numbers of cruisers, destroyers, corvettes and other craft. The constant flashes from their guns indicated that the beach was getting a heavy pounding.

"Behind this advance brigade stretching in a never-ending stream across the Channel, came line after line of L.C.T.s landing craft, tanks escorted by corvettes and P.T. boats.

"We were never attacked by enemy airplanes although the sky was terrific. Second Lieut. Benson, of Iowa, said: "The Channel was fairly calm and the boats bounced along smoothly. Ships and many were towing barrage balloons."

Colonel William Schwartz added: "When I arrived over the beach our battleships brought their fire to bear on the shore."

78 **Front page of the Evening Standard, Tuesday 6 June 1944**

At noon Churchill gave his first report to the House of Commons - and with it much public reassurance - on what he described as an operation which was

> the most complicated and difficult that has ever taken place. It involves tides, winds, waves, visibility, both from the air and the sea standpoint, and the combined employment of land, air, and sea forces in the highest degree of intimacy and in contact with conditions which could not and cannot be fully foreseen....The battle that has now begun will grow constantly in scale and in intensity for many weeks to come, and I shall not attempt to speculate upon its course. This I may say however. Complete unity prevails throughout the Allied Armies. There is a brotherhood in arms between us and our friends of the United States. There is complete confidence in the Supreme Commander, General Eisenhower, and his lieutenants, and also in the commander of the Expeditionary Force, General Montgomery. The ardour and spirit of the troops, as I saw myself, embarking in these last few days was splendid to witness. Nothing that equipment, science or forethought could do has been neglected, and the whole process of opening this great new front will be pursued with the utmost resolution both by the commanders and by the United States and British Governments whom they serve.[11]

D-Day Battle Front

Over in Field Marshal Rommel's headquarters at La Roche-Guyon, his Chief of Staff, General Hans Speidel, chose the evening of 5 June for a dinner party. His guests included a number of senior officers and German civilian officials. According to one, whilst the allied invasion fleet approached the French coast, the conversation was animated. They touched on many topics such as events in Italy and Russia, French politics and Hitler's future plans, rather than the threat of any allied attack. It seems to have been a most enjoyable occasion with a pleasant after dinner stroll in the château grounds. A telephone call in the early hours of 6 June broke the news: the German 7th Army HQ reported allied paratroop landings. The party came to an abrupt end.

On board the invasion fleet tossing in the rough seas, much study was being given to the final operation orders marked 'Top Secret' and 'Not To Be Taken Ashore'. They had been able to open these only after the final order to sail had been given. At last true maps of the landing areas had been issued, finally revealing the destination - so long hidden under the enigmatic description `The Far Shore' - as the coast of Normandy, stretching along the beaches of Calvados and around to the Cherbourg peninsula.

Post-war searches of captured German intelligence files showed the degree of success of allied security and deception measures. In over 200 reports from German agents in many different countries only one had mentioned Normandy as a possible allied landing place, and even that had been filed away as of no consequence.

In the landings now about to take place the troops which had either trained or waited in West Sussex for this momentous day were to play their key role on the battle front ahead.

A and B Squadrons of the 13/18th Hussars in their DD Sherman tanks were given the task of landing seven minutes before H-Hour (7 a.m.) on Sword Beach. They were to support the 3rd Infantry Division's 8th Brigade, the first infantry ashore on Sword Beach and the same battalions which had so recently rehearsed this role on the sands at Climping.

The operation order of the 13/18th Hussars laid down that after the tanks had been launched and had achieved 'touch down' (i.e. had grounded) they should engage enemy targets on the beach from a range of about 400 yards whilst still in the water. This was to gain fire superiority over the beaches to cover the landing of the vehicles of the 79th Armoured Division's assault engineers, and to assist the infantry to move forward.

The regiment's third sabre, or fighting squadron - C Squadron - was to land from tank landing craft and support the 1st Battalion Suffolk Regiment in an attack upon two enemy strongholds known as Morris and Hillman.

The operation order instructed that 'The greatest boldness and initiative will be shown and the attack will be pressed home'. The DD tanks must not be abandoned unless actually sinking. During the crossing from England there had been considerable doubt whether it would be possible to launch the DDs in the rough seas at all. The code-word Floater was received at sea indicating that Brigadier Prior-Palmer, commanding the 27th Armoured Brigade, had decided that the tank landing in the sea would go ahead as planned.

When the tank landing craft reached their launching position about 5,000 yards from Sword Beach at 6.15 in the morning, a Force 5 wind was blowing. Thirty-one tanks were successfully launched and cruised round in a circle before starting their run-in to the beach. The regimental historian recorded that 'everybody had formed a pretty good idea....that the sea was not calm, but, by the time they had been in the water a few minutes, they were left with no doubt whatever that the sea was very rough'.[12]

79 **Sword Beach**
The first wave of troops comes ashore on D-Day. Some fall wounded by machine gun and mortar fire. In the background, through a haze of smoke, are landing craft and tanks of the 13/18th Royal Hussars, only a few days earlier camped in Petworth Park.

Despite these conditions one DD crew member recalled that 'The run-in over the last few miles was wonderful - nothing happening at all, except that as the light became stronger we could see the entire ocean was covered by lines of vessels, elbow to elbow and seemingly stretching back to the U.K.'. The same soldier remarked on the extraordinary degree of confidence achieved by the crews in what he described as nearly fifty tons of metal and explosives kept afloat by a mixture of canvas and pram struts. [13]

Out of the thirty-four DDs launched, thirty-one reached 'touch down' despite the adverse weather conditions. This feat alone has attracted a considerable number of compliments about the crew's seamanship. Of the three that did not survive the run-in, one sank when its propeller was not engaged, and two were accidentally rammed and sunk by landing craft. The possible dangers the DD crews faced were graphically illustrated by the fate that befell twenty-nine American DDs launched off Omaha Beach. Of these, twenty-two were almost immediately swamped and sunk by the waves and five destroyed by enemy fire.

Once in their 'touch down' positions the A and B Squadron tanks opened fire on all possible targets on the beach and were credited with having destroyed within thirty minutes three or four 75 mm guns and four or five 50 mm, as well as numerous smaller 20 mm guns. By twenty minutes after H-Hour enemy fire on the beach is said to have been reduced to that of snipers only.

As the rising tide swept in, some of the DDs were swamped and had to be abandoned. In some cases crews continued to keep firing even as the water began to flood their turrets. They escaped by means of small emergency dinghies carried in each tank. Together with the Crab, or flail, tanks of the 22nd Dragoons - which suffered considerable loss in mine clearing - the DDs of the 13/18th Hussars made a major contribution in keeping British casualties on Sword Beach to a figure well below the level feared.

Curiously, in view of the regiment's temporary association with Petworth during the D-Day build-up, just a week from D-Day the tide of battle carried the Hussars to the small Normandy town of Ranville, near Caen, to which by chance many years later Petworth was twinned.

The East Riding Yeomanry - also from Petworth Park camp - landed some time after H-Hour to assist the 3rd Division's 9th Brigade in clearing German coastal defences a little inland and joined in what the 27th Armoured Brigade's war diary described as the 'rather sticky battle' in progress.

One Yeomanry officer later recalled waking to the throbbing of his landing craft's diesel engines as it made its way through the heaving sea, and to the oily stench and the sound of someone being sick. He found it hard to believe he was not on another exercise but for the fear in the pit of his stomach and the notes about German defences and photographs of beaches littering the greasy floor.

As the landing craft approached the French coast 'wreathed and flown with smoke-tattered flags of the explosion and burning of buildings....the men and steel striving for Ouistreham....dying and shooting under the smoke clouds drifting across the Orne, we were watching the newsreel of the harsh forefront of world events which we were making. A fighter fell burning from the grey cloud-base and slowly dropped the other side of the river. What we had read about and prepared and trained for and thought about was here, with only a little strip of the neutrality of the sea between us and our first work in action. War had come to us and to me.'

THE LONGEST DAY

He wrote of the regiment's first action after it had landed that day: 'We went on into the nearest battle, into the streams of red tracer and the vicious crack of the anti-tank shell and the hammer-clarion of the screaming shell that arrives for you and the sad pyres of burning tanks blowing up with yesterday's comrades.'[14]

A former private of the 8th Brigade's 1st Battalion Suffolk Regiment has memories that must have been shared by many of the brigade's three infantry battalions that came in with the first assault wave on Sword Beach.

He has recalled how, trembling and with rifle tightly clenched, he had crouched waiting as his landing craft had edged in between others. Some of the craft were burning.

He heard the engines reverse as the bows of the vessel grounded and there was a shout of 'ramps down'. Determined not to make himself a target at the top of the ramp, as soon as the order came he jumped from the craft into the cold water up to his chest. Holding his rifle high he waded as quickly as he could to the dry beach.[15]

80 **Commandos Ashore**
Commandos of 1st Special Service Brigade led by Lord Lovat and his personal piper, Bill Millin, land at Hermanville-sur-Mer on Sword Beach on D-Day. In the background are Sherman tanks of the 13/18th Royal Hussars. These commandos had been quartered at Lavington House and Burton Park.

Also landing on Sword Beach was the 1st Special Service Brigade commanded by Lord Lovat, a brigade which in the build-up had been stationed in West and East Sussex. With brigade headquarters at Lavington House and Burton Park, both not far from Petworth, No. 3 Commando was at Worthing, No. 4 at Bexhill, No. 6 at Hove, and No. 45 (Royal Marine) Commando in the Petworth district.

As Lord Lovat's personal piper, Bill Millin, waded ashore in water up to his shoulders, Lord Lovat reportedly shouted 'Give us *Highland Laddie*, man!'. Obediently the piper played as he splashed ashore. Then, as the commandos landed and with a beach still under spasmodic mortar and sniper fire, he paraded up and down by the edge of the water playing *The Road to the Isles*. Later Millin and his pipes were again prominent when Lord Lovat led No. 4 Commando to the famous link-up with the glider-borne troops of the 6th Airborne Division who had seized the vital Pegasus Bridge over the Orne Canal. His pipes played a pre-arranged recognition signal between the commandos and the airborne force.

West of Sword Beach landed Numbers 41 and 48 (Royal Marine) Commandos of the 4th Special Service Brigade whose headquarters had been in Cowdray Park, Midhurst, during the build-up. A further unit of the brigade, No. 47 (Royal Marine) Commando, landed on the extreme right flank of

THE LONGEST DAY

the British assault on the edge of the 50th Infantry Division's Gold Beach. Here it had the formidable task of trying to reach the village of Port-en-Bessin through no less than seven miles of enemy-held territory. Despite the tremendous battering the German defenders had suffered from pre H-Hour air and naval bombardment, the commandos engaged in severe fighting with considerable casualties in attacking German strongpoints and in `mopping-up' operations along the coastal defence belt.

British Commando
Combined Operations

No. 6 Beach Group, some of whose units had been in Petworth Park, faced a difficult and dangerous landing. A concrete enemy gun emplacement, with a field of fire commanding the whole of its area, survived for a considerable time, ultimately forcing the transfer of the group's personnel and stores to an adjacent beach.

81 **Cycling Canadians**
Troops of the 9th Canadian Brigade wade ashore in the late morning of D-Day at Bernières-sur-Mer on Juno Beach. The plan was to reach Caen by nightfall on bicycle. One month earlier these same troops had rehearsed this landing at Bracklesham.

The Staffordshire Yeomanry, the third armoured regiment of the 27th Armoured Brigade, advanced ten miles inland to Caen for one of the most dramatic battles of the historic day. The daring - but unsuccessful - attempt to capture the city by nightfall turned into a major obstacle and did massive damage to Montgomery's reputation, especially with his American allies. [16]

The plan for the 3rd Division's 185th Brigade, made up of the 2nd Battalion The King's Shropshire Light Infantry (KSLI), the 1st Battalion The Royal Norfolk Regiment, and the 2nd Battalion The Royal Warwickshire Regiment, was to advance swiftly on Caen from the village of Hermanville, just inland from Sword Beach, with the KSLI riding down the main road on the Staffordshire Yeomanry's tanks.

82 Juno Beach
*Tanks and infantry of the
3rd Canadian Infantry Division
and 2nd Canadian Armoured
Brigade make their D-Day
landing. Some had practised
this landfall at Bracklesham
a month earlier.*

83 The Advance
*British infantry prepare to advance inland from Sword Beach on D-Day. The first landings on Sword were made
by the 3rd Infantry Division, 27th Armoured Brigade, and several Marine and Commando Corps.*

An exceptionally high morning tide on Sword Beach presented the first problem, leaving only a narrow beach, in places ten yards wide, for unloading the mass of tanks and transports that followed the initial assault forces. There was immense congestion and serious delays.

Despite such difficulties the KSLI, operating on foot and supported by one squadron of the Staffordshires, managed to penetrate to within two miles of Caen, their advance halted by the tanks of the crack German 21st Panzer Division. 'Few could have equalled their effort; no one could have done more' wrote one commentator. [17] The timetable had gone drastically awry and the plan to capture the city, a major key in allied strategy, had failed, 'preventing the Allies from moving inland and keeping the British pinned so close to their landing beaches that after a month of fighting, battleships off the coast could still add the fire of their big guns in support of infantry in the front lines'. [18]

The battle for Caen now degenerated into a bitter and bloody ordeal of house-to-house fighting and it was not until 18 July that German resistance was broken and the city fell into allied hands.

Aftermath

For the troops the initial D-Day assault marked the start of active service which was to last, interspersed by short periods of rest, for eleven more months until the final German surrender in May 1945.

The 27th Armoured Brigade was itself disbanded towards the end of the Normandy campaign, but its component regiments and other units continued to fight on in other formations until final victory.

For two months after D-Day the 1st and 4th Special Service Brigades protected the eastern flank of the British bridgehead along the Orne. In the autumn of 1944 the 4th took a leading part in the stiff fighting around the Scheldt estuary to clear the approaches to the vital strategic port of Antwerp. After a brief return to West Sussex in August 1944 the 1st took part in the winter campaign in Holland and then the crossing of the Rhine in March 1945.

**15th Scottish
Infantry Division**

The 15th Scottish Division suffered heavy casualties in its first major action, part of Operation Epsom launched by the 8th Corps on 26 June 1944 to seize a bridgehead over the Odon. The crossing, through a rocky ravine, cost more British lives than the crossing of the Rhine the following year. But its fine performance earned special congratulations from Montgomery, and it was to achieve distinction again by its resolute stand against a counter-attack by elements of four SS Panzer Divisions on 1 July. This left the German High Command fearing that the war in the West was already lost. At the end of July the division also played a leading part in Operation Bluecoat, the British offensive accompanying the American break-out from the base of the Cherbourg peninsula. It was also to have a prominent role in the Reichwald Forest fighting in early 1945 and in the subsequent crossing of the Rhine.

The 4th Armoured Brigade was heavily engaged in the battle of the Falaise 'pocket' where German forces were trapped as they tried to escape the allied advance in August 1944. The specialised armour of the 79th Armoured Division continued to play a vital part in all major British attacks during the Normandy campaign, particularly where strong fixed enemy defences were encountered.

Casualties

Although British casualties on D-Day were much lower than some estimates had forecast, they were still heavy. Before the end of the first day's assault the 2nd Battalion of The East Yorkshire Regiment suffered 200 casualties after its Sword Beach landing. Between D-Day and mid-September 40,000 allied troops were killed and some 160,000 wounded in the battle for Normandy. [19] The treatment of casualties was a crucial part of D-Day planning.

At the beginning of the war the government established an Emergency Medical Service (EMS). Ten EMS hutted wards of forty beds each, primarily for wartime casualties, were built at St. Richards Hospital in Chichester, bringing the total number of beds up to 594. A further five EMS hutted wards were put up at the Royal West Sussex Hospital, also in Chichester, taking their bed total to 314. The number of beds was therefore increased dramatically.

As preparations for the invasion built up, St. Richards, in common with many other hospitals along the South Coast, drastically reduced its numbers of civilian patients, making ready to receive the expected wounded troops from France. Two wards at the West Sussex County Mental Hospital at Graylingwell in Chichester were also brought into use for D-Day casualties, and beds in the EMS hutted wards at St. Richards were set aside for German prisoners-of-war. Eric Skilton was on the administrative staff of St. Richards during the war and has a vivid recollection of the time:

> The most outstanding period was the sudden evacuation of all hospital patients inland to various hospitals, which made us soon realize that D-Day was approaching. Doctors and nursing staff were doubled by the arrival of the complete staff from the West Middlesex Hospital and a unit of Canadian Army medical personnel who took over several offices and stores. For several days we were engaged in rolling bandages and packing them in sterilising drums; all the wards had their beds piled high with prepared dressings and surgical equipment.

> The hutted wards were made ready to accommodate enemy troops and civilians captured at the initial stages of the D-Day landings. Then it all happened - suddenly there was a hive of activity. *Southdown* coaches had been converted into ambulances by the removal of all seats, and stretcher slings had been made by hanging straps from the coach roof, and using the floor space for other wounded on stretchers.

> The first casualties arrived straight off the beaches of France. Some horrific sights, and in most cases soaking wet, some not even making the beach! 300 at a time, and every type of regiment and corps, captured German military, and various civilian nationalities including White Russians, forced labour gangs and French women living with or married to Germans who had been shooting at our forces. The prisoners were sent to Graylingwell.

> Within twenty-four hours all available space was taken up, even the corridor floors were lined with the wounded. Treated wounds were dressed on the spot and the more seriously injured kept for major surgery. Minor cases were transferred the same day to hospitals inland, as far away as Basingstoke. German military were placed in the hutted wards and guarded by a solitary soldier sitting in the middle of the ward with tin hat and fixed bayonet!

THE LONGEST DAY

As a young lad I was tremendously impressed by the spirit and courage of our forces.
I remember one Royal Marine sitting up in bed having had a bullet enter under his jaw,
removing part of his tongue and coming out at the side of his cheek. Yet he managed to
joke and asked me to let his family know that he was OK! [20]

Whilst the most severely wounded from the Normandy fighting were given immediate treatment on
landing back in this country, those less seriously hurt were sent on from Portsmouth to Chichester
where they arrived every forty-eight hours or so. When sufficiently recovered they were either
sent home or transferred to convalescent centres.

Pat Saunders was then a young van boy working for the Central Laundry in Broyle Road,
Chichester, which dealt with the laundry from St. Richards and from the Forest Hospital at
Horsham, the Canadian No. 1 General Hospital. Bed linen and uniforms came into the laundry
every day, but by D-Day this increased to twice a day, and as the casualties were received from
Normandy a night shift had to be started to cope with the extra workload.

He visited St. Richards regularly and saw the wounded invasion troops and the German prisoners-
of-war as they were brought in on board the converted coaches carrying fourteen to sixteen
patients at a time. The local doctors had extra help from RAF and army doctors when available. Mr.
Saunders remembers that on occasions a surgical team would be sent down from St. Bartholomews
Hospital in London under the charge of Mr. Rupert Corbett, a surgeon. Hard-pressed nursing staff
would also be relieved at times by nurses evacuated from London hospitals. [21]

Casualties continued to arrive in Chichester for some weeks after D-Day and the pressure did not
ease on St. Richards and its staff until a sufficient number of field hospitals had been set up in
France.

Flora MacDonald Brown (now Roberts) was a member of the Queen Alexandra's Imperial Military
Nursing Service (the QAs) in the 23rd British General Hospital. Her unit spent the early summer of
1944 at Goodwood House, just outside Chichester, packing its tented hospital ready for action in
France:

> The wards - big marquees - were all packed in such a way that as soon as they were
> unrolled and erected they were ready to function, i.e. medical wards complete, and surgical
> wards with theatres and equipment ready to perform operations. We were a completely
> tented hospital.

> Being at the front of the house we were aware of great activity, with a great deal of despatch
> riders arriving and departing with urgent messages. We heard a rumour that `it was to be
> on' on the 5th, then the rumour was denied, but in the early hours of the 6th there was a
> great deal of noise, and motor cycles roaring up and down that lovely drive, and we knew
> this was it.

> The next morning a few of us went for a walk to the green hill set behind the house. It was a
> beautiful, glorious sunny day, and as we lay on the grass we heard and then saw some
> planes approaching, very low, and passing overhead. It was then we realized that there was
> a glider attached to each plane, and that there were hundreds and hundreds of them.
> Goodwood was bang under the flight path of these invasion planes, and it was a very

sobering and frightening sensation as we realized that each of these gliders was full of young men who were to be cut loose over Normandy and left to drift down to a very uncertain landing. It still makes me shiver to think of it, and to realize that many never even reached the ground or fired a gun.

The QAs remained at Goodwood until 24 June, and each day as their work was done, they would wander around the estate enjoying the beauty of its woods and hills. They had picnics on the lawn to which they invited servicemen from RAF Tangmere and army units stationed nearby. When they left they moved to a holding area in woods near Southampton for embarkation four days later. Their tented hospital was erected on the outskirts of Bayeux and there the wounded were given immediate emergency treatment before being flown across the Channel to hospitals in the South of England.[22]

84 **Goodwood Nurses**
Queen Alexandra's Nurses,
23rd British General Hospital,
pictured outside their
Goodwood House base,
well protected from blast by
brick walls and sandbags,
17 June 1944.
One week later they left to
set up a tented field hospital
near Bayeux.

85 **Nurses' Picnic**
The QAs picnic on the lawns
at Goodwood shortly before
their move to France.

Victory Assured

D-Day was a turning point in the Second World War, the success of the Normandy landings paving the way for the liberation of Europe. By the end of August 1944 Paris had been liberated and although the long march to Berlin lay ahead, soon over five years of war were to come to an end on VE-Day - 8 May 1945.

Now, fifty years after D-Day, the visible reminders of the greatest seaborne invasion in history are largely confined to the wrecked sections of Mulberry Harbours and to the crumbling gun emplacements on the Normandy coastline. These prefabricated harbours and gun sites symbolise the central parts of the campaign - the enormous task of organisation and preparation and the massive challenge that faced the allied invasion force.

86 **'Bolo' Whistler** *General Montgomery with Brigadier Lashmer Gordon ('Bolo') Whistler, for twenty-six years an officer in The Royal Sussex Regiment. Soon after D-Day he was to succeed Major-General Tom Rennie in command of the 3rd Infantry Division on the road to victory from Normandy to Bremen.*

87 **Victory at Hand**
Prime Minister Winston Churchill in the uniform of Honorary Colonel of the 5th (Cinque Ports) Battalion, The Royal Sussex Regiment, on his visit to 3rd Division HQ, 23 March 1945, a few days before the Rhine crossing. Prominently displayed is the five-pointed white star painted on the sides and top of all allied invasion vehicles for ground/air recognition.

D-Day Remembered

The story of the build-up and landings of D-Day has been told in countless books and by museums on both sides of the Channel, but the role played by West Sussex has been almost entirely overlooked by historians, even though its geographical position ensured its prominence as an invasion springboard.

Hopefully the story told here will have gone some way towards describing the contribution of local people and places to these great events, and specifying the parts played in the invasion by air and land forces based in West Sussex during these crucial months.

This book is the result of research in both national and local archives. To the written sources have been added the memories of those then either living or serving in the county, people involved in some way or other with what was going on all around them as the drama unfolded. Their story is largely told here for the first time.

A measure of the success in compiling this record is that an archive of D-Day recollections has now been started for permanent preservation in the West Sussex Record Office. The archive continues to grow and it is hoped that this book may encourage others to add their own memories to the story of West Sussex in the build-up to D-Day and the Normandy landings as a fitting tribute to this momentous period fifty years ago.

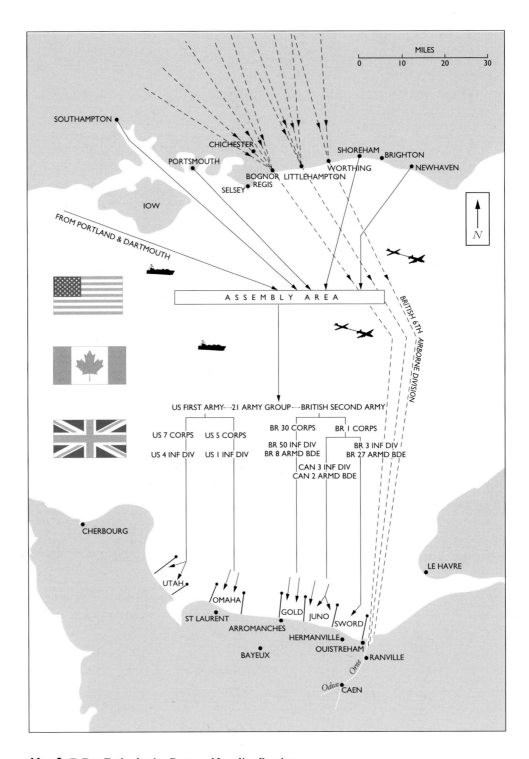

Map 2 *D-Day Embarkation Ports and Landing Beaches*

D-Day Army Units in West Sussex

The following list is an attempt to show the location of army units throughout the county in the build-up to D-Day on 6 June 1944. In this present context the county includes the mid-Sussex area formerly in East Sussex, but since 1974 transferred to West Sussex by local government reorganisation.

The information is derived from official sources supplemented by personal reminiscences. It is not definitive and any additions or comments will be welcomed by the West Sussex Record Office.

Abbreviations used:

RA	Royal Artillery
RAMC	Royal Army Medical Corps
RAOC	Royal Army Ordnance Corps
RASC	Royal Army Service Corps
RE	Royal Engineers
REME	Royal Electrical and Mechanical Engineers

Angmering

75th General Hospital, RAMC.

Ardingly

8th Corps HQ (Wakehurst Place).
Staffordshire Yeomanry,
27th Armoured Brigade (Wakehurst Place).

Arundel

188th Field Artillery Group, US Army.
951st Battalion Field Artillery, US Army.
105th Medical Battalion, APO 30, US Army.

Barlavington

1st Special Service Brigade,
Junior Officers' Mess (Burton Park).

Billingshurst

1st Corps Troops HQ
(Inglefield Manor, Five Oaks).
3rd Infantry Troops Workshops
(Inglefield Manor, Five Oaks).
13th Medium Regiment, RA (Five Oaks).
67th Medium Regiment, RA (Woodale).
16th Casualty Clearing Station, RAMC
(Five Oaks).
44th, 45th Ordnance Ammunition Companies,
RASC (Five Oaks).
10th Port Operating Company, RE
(Rosier Farm, tented camp).
1025th Port Operating Company, RE (Tedfold).
1028th Port Operating Company, RE
(Woodale).

Bognor Regis

8th Hussars.
120th Infantry Regiment, 30th US Infantry
Division, HQ (Victoria Hotel).
117th Road Construction Company, RE
(Royal Hotel).
634th Tank Destroyer Battalion, US Army
(seafront hotels and guest houses).

Bolney
Marshalling Camp (Wykehurst Park).

Boxgrove
6th, 23rd, 121st General Hospitals,
RAMC (Goodwood House).
5th, 6th Maxillo-Facial Surgical Teams
(Goodwood House).
3rd Chest Surgery Surgical Team
(Goodwood House).
227th Field Park Company, RE
(Halnaker House).

Chichester
36th Beach Group (Barracks).
Beach Recovery Sections, RAOC (Barracks).
10 Inter-Allied Commando.
18th Battalion, The Durham Light Infantry
(Barracks).
112th Field Regiment, RA.
30th US Infantry Division Command Post
(Barracks).

Cowfold
15th Scottish Infantry Division, REME, HQ
(Clock House).

Crawley - see **Worth**

Cuckfield
Marshalling Camp (Borde Hill).

Easebourne
4th Special Service Brigade HQ (Cowdray Park).

East Lavington
1st Special Service Brigade HQ
(Lavington House [now Seaford College]).

East Preston
15th Scottish Infantry Division,
Reconnaissance Regiment
(Court House, Normandy Drive).

Felpham
3rd Battalion, 120th Infantry Regiment,
30th US Infantry Division.

Findon
2nd Battalion,
The Argyll and Sutherland Highlanders,
227th Highland Infantry Brigade
(Cissbury, tented camp).
2nd Battalion, The Gordon Highlanders,
227th Highland Infantry Brigade
(Muntham Court, tented camp).

Funtington
Canadian troops.
Note that an RAF medical unit was based here:
the 53rd RAF Mobile Field Hospital was in a
tented camp at West Ashling House.

Goodwood - see **Boxgrove**

Haywards Heath - see **Cuckfield**

Horsham
Port Construction and Repair Groups
(Denne Park, tented camp).
80th Anti-Aircraft Brigade, RA
(Broadbridge Heath).
86th Heavy Regiment, RA.
11th Bulk Petrol Company, RASC
(Denne Park).
Note that a total of fifteen Construction and
Lines of Communications Units passed through
Denne Park camps.

Itchingfield
79th Armoured Division HQ (Muntham).
9th General Transport (Amphibious) Company,
RASC (Barns Green).

Kirdford
91st Field Company, RE.
21st Beach Reconnaissance Section
(Roundwyck House).
Beach Recovery Section, RAOC
(Roundwyck House).

Littlehampton
X Troop, 10 Inter-Allied Commando.
17th Field Company, RE, 3rd Infantry Division
(Beach Hotel).
71st Field Company, RE, 3rd Infantry Division
(Dorset House).

Littlehampton (continued)
Embarkation HQ (Arun View Hotel).
6th Pioneer Group HQ (Roland House).

Lodsworth
Tank battalion, British Army
(common near Snapelands Farm).

Lower Beeding
15th Scottish Infantry Division Workshops.
101st, 224th Field Companies, RE.

Middleton-on-Sea
185th Infantry Brigade HQ, 3rd Infantry
Division (Middleton Manor, tented camp).
Note that a total of fifteen Service and Lines of
Communications Units of the 30th Corps
passed through Middleton-on-Sea.

Midhurst - *see* **Easebourne**

Nuthurst
103rd Heavy Anti-Aircraft Regiment, RA.

Parham
20th Field Company, RE, 15th Scottish Infantry
Division (Parham Park).
278th, 279th Field Companies, RE
(Parham Park).

Petworth
27th Armoured Brigade HQ
(Limbo Farm).
27th Armoured Brigade Field Park Company
(Beechfield).
27th Armoured Brigade Workshop
(Flathurst Stables).

Petworth Park No. 1 Camp
(near Pheasant Copse)
1st Squadron, 22nd Dragoons,
30th Armoured Brigade.
260th, 262nd, 267th Forward Delivery
Squadrons.
71st Army Field Company, RE.

Petworth Park No. 2 Camp
(off Upperton Road)
13/18th Royal Hussars (Queen Mary's Own),
27th Armoured Brigade.

Petworth Park No. 2 Camp (continued)
East Riding Yeomanry, 27th Armoured Brigade.
1st Squadron, Lothians and Border Horse,
30th Armoured Brigade.

Petworth Park No. 3 Camp
(Lower Pond area)
1st Battalion, Buckinghamshire Light Infantry,
The Oxfordshire and Buckinghamshire Light
Infantry.
74th Army Field Company, RE.
Note that in this camp were also
RAF and RN units:
55th, 102nd Balloon Sections, Royal Air Force,
and Royal Naval Commandos.

Petworth Park camp numbers unknown
11th Light Field Ambulance, 27th Armoured
Brigade.
90th Company, RASC, 27th Armoured Brigade.
Signals Squadron, 27th Armoured Brigade.
6th Beach Group HQ.
238th Petrol Depot.
45th (Royal Marine) Commando.
20th Port Detachment, RAMC.
227th Field Park Company, RE.
90th US Army Air Corps.

Pulborough
131st Field Regiment, RA, 15th Division.

Rudgwick
51st Heavy Regiment, RA
(Gaskins House, Bucks Green).

Rustington
116th Wireless Intelligence Section, Intelligence
Corps (Millfield Hospital, Sea Lane;
Convalescent Home and Xylophone House,
Sea Road).
2nd Company, Pioneer Corps
(Cudlow House, Sea Lane).
102nd Company, Pioneer Corps.
308th Company, Pioneer Corps
(Mount Rowland School, Station Road).
93rd Light Anti-Aircraft Regiment, RA.

APPENDIX ONE

Shipley

Armoured unit, Canadian Army
(Lackenhurst, Brooks Green).
15th Scottish Infantry Division HQ
(Knepp Castle).

Singleton

4th US Cavalry HQ (Grove House).
4th US Cavalry (hutted camp).

Slinfold

313th Company, Pioneer Corps
(Buckman Corner camp).
73rd Light Anti-Aircraft Regiment, RA.
264th Special Delivery Squadron.

Stansted

3rd British Infantry Division,
Free French and Canadian units
(Transit Camp A1, Stansted Park).

Steyning

Royal Marine Engineer Commando
(Chantry Green House).

Storrington

624th Field Park Company, RE (Greyfriars).
44th Lowland Brigade, 15th Scottish Infantry
Division Workshop (Merrywood).

Sullington

2nd Anti-Aircraft Group School
(Barns Farm camp).

Westbourne

US Infantry (Atchards, tented camp).
Army camp (Monks Hill woods).

Wiston

227th Highland Infantry Brigade,
15th Scottish Infantry Division, HQ
(Wiston House).
10th Battalion, The Highland Light Infantry,
227th Highland Infantry Brigade
(Wiston Park, tented camp).
97th Anti-Tank Regiment, RA,
15th Scottish Infantry Division (Weppons).

Worth

8th Corps HQ (The Grove).
8th Corps Rear HQ (Worth Priory).
30th Corps HQ
(Milton Mount College, Three Bridges).
10th Survey Regiment, RA (Tilgate House).

Worthing

4th Armoured Brigade HQ
(Eardley House Hotel, Marine Parade;
Armandale, Down View Road; '
95 Grand Parade; Crossways, 22 Mill Road).
The Royal Scots Greys, 4th Armoured Brigade
(The Steyne and adjacent houses).
The 3rd County of London Yeomanry,
4th Armoured Brigade
(2 Chatham Road and adjacent houses).
44th Battalion, The Royal Tank Regiment,
4th Armoured Brigade (Winchelsea House,
Winchelsea Gardens and adjacent houses).
2nd Battalion, The King's Royal Rifle Corps,
4th Armoured Brigade (Drill Hall, Forest Road).
4th Armoured Brigade Workshop
(51 Chesswood Road).
44th Lowland Infantry Brigade,
15th Scottish Infantry Division, HQ
(Beach Hotel).
7th Battalion, The King's Own Scottish
Borderers, 44th Lowland Brigade
(48 Crescent Road).
6th Battalion, The Royal Scots Fusiliers,
44th Lowland Brigade (3 Heene Road).
8th Battalion, The Royal Scots
(The Royal Regiment),
44th Lowland Brigade (Wellington House).
No. 3 Commando (Broadwater Road).
181st Field Regiment, RA,
15th Scottish Infantry Division
(Offington House, Warren Road).
59th Medium Regiment, RA
(Winchelsea House, Winchelsea Gardens).
72nd Medium Regiment, RA
(Drill Hall, Forest Road).
14th Field Ambulance, RAMC
(Warnes Hotel, Marine Parade).
737th Artillery Company, RASC (Warnes
Hotel, Eardley House Hotel, Marine Parade).

D-Day Airfields,
Advanced Landing Grounds and
Air Observation Post Airstrips
in West Sussex

This information lists the Royal Air Force, Dominion and other squadrons operational on D-Day, 6 June 1944, with their main duties, and is based on three printed sources:

Chris Ashworth,
Action Stations 9: Military airfields of the Central South and South-East
(Wellingborough, Patrick Stephens, 1985);

Robin J. Brooks,
Sussex Airfields in the Second World War
(Newbury, Countryside Books, 1993);

Ken Rimell,
Merlin & the Sabre:
The Story of Royal Air Force Apuldram 1943-1945
(Apuldram, the author, 1992), p.34.

Abbreviations used:

RAAF   Royal Australian Air Force
RCAF   Royal Canadian Air Force
RNZAF Royal New Zealand Air Force

AIRFIELDS
Ford

125 Wing: RAAF squadrons 132 (City of Bombay); 453; 602 (City of Glasgow) flying the Spitfire IX.

144 Wing: RAAF squadron 456 flying the Mosquito XVII.
RCAF squadrons 441 (Silver Fox); 442 (Caribou); 443 (Hornet) flying the Spitfire IX.

Cover for the landing craft in the Channel and on the landing beaches. Sorties inland to prevent enemy bombers and fighters attacking the beaches. Note that RAF Ford commanded the Littlehampton Air Sea Rescue Station, partly based at Littlehampton Golf Club.

Merston

145 Wing: Free French squadrons 329 (GC I/2 Cigones); 340 (GC IV/2 Ile de France); 341 (GC III/2 Alsace) flying the Spitfire IX.

Low level cover for troop-carrying vessels and over the landing beaches.

Shoreham

141 Wing: Free French squadron 345 flying the Spitfire VB.

277 Air Sea Rescue squadron flying the Sea Otter.

Cover for the landings and escort for the air-tug/glider combinations carrying airborne troops.

Tangmere

126 Wing: RCAF squadrons 401; 411; 412 flying the Spitfire IX.

127 Wing: RCAF squadrons 403; 416 (City of Oshawa); 421 flying the Spitfire IX.

Cover across the Channel, the landing beaches and for forward troops inland.

APPENDIX TWO

Thorney Island

123 Wing: 198, 609 squadrons flying the
Typhoon IB.

136 Wing: 164, 183 squadrons flying the
Typhoon IB.

Ground attack sweeps concentrating on enemy
armour.

Westhampnett

129 Wing: 184 squadron flying the Typhoon IB.

Ground attack on German strongpoints and gun
positions.

ADVANCED LANDING GROUNDS
Apuldram

134 Wing: Czech squadrons 310; 312
(Wilenski); 313 flying the Spitfire IX.

Cover for the landing beaches. 'Apuldram
carried out more sorties that day than any
other R.A.F. Station' (Rimell, p.22).

Bognor

132 Wing: 66 squadron; Norwegian squadrons
331; 332 flying the Spitfire IX.

Cover for the landing beaches and attacks on
German rocket V-I launch sites.

Coolham

133 Wing: 129 (Mysore) squadron; Polish
squadrons 306 (Torun); 315 (Deblin) flying the
Mustang III.

Escort for the air-tug/glider combinations
carrying airborne troops.

Funtington

122 Wing: squadrons 19; 65 (East India); 122
(Bombay) flying the Mustang III.

Cover for the landing beaches.

Selsey

135 Wing: squadron 222 (Natal);
Belgian squadron 349; RNZAF squadron 485
flying the Spitfire IX.

Cover for the landing beaches.

AIR OBSERVATION POST AIRSTRIPS
East Grinstead

(Hammerwood, Forest Row, East Sussex)
659 Air Observation Post squadron flying the
Auster Mark IV.
D-Day duties not known.

Parham

Believed to be operational with Auster spotter
aircraft, but details not known.

SOURCES

TEXT REFERENCES

Chapter 1

1   David Eisenhower, *Eisenhower: at War 1943-1945* (London, Collins, 1986), p. 251.

2   Max Hastings, *Overlord: D-Day and the Battle for Normandy* (London, Michael Joseph, 1984), p. 26.

3   Hastings, p. 34.

Chapter 2

1   Ronald Atkin, *Dieppe 1942: The Jubilee Disaster* (London, Macmillan, 1980), p. 252.

2   West Sussex Record Office (WSRO), MP 3730.

3   Lieutenant-Colonel R.M.P. Carver, *Second to None: The Royal Scots Greys - 1919-1945* (Glasgow, McCorquodale, 1954), p. 108.

4   WSRO, MP 3730.

5   Carver, p. 108.

6   WSRO, MP 3730.

7   *Bognor Regis Post,* 1 January 1966.

8   WSRO, MP 3730.

9   'A Scrapbook of Items concerning Middleton-on-Sea.' [Compiled by the Women's Institute, 1957-67.] In custody of Middleton-on-Sea WI.

10   WSRO, MP 1745.

11   WSRO, MP 3730.

12   Rex Williams, *You Must Remember This* [Crawley in World War Two] (Balcombe, Rural Rides Publications, 1992), p. 49.

13   Arundel Castle Archives, Estate Office Papers (uncatalogued).

14   Public Record Office (PRO), DEFE 2/997.

15   *Daily Express,* 24 October 1946.

16   V.C. Ellison, *Europe Revisited. The East Riding Yeomanry in the Liberation of Europe and the Defeat of Germany* (Hull, A. Brown [1946]), p. 6.

Chapter 3

1   Lieutenant-General H.G. Martin, *The History of the Fifteenth Scottish Division 1939-1945* (Edinburgh, Blackwood, 1948), pp. 23-4.

2   PRO, WO 171/1300.

3   Information from Irene MacDonald of Wiston.

4   WSRO, MP 3730.

5   Stephen Badsey, *D-Day from the Normandy Beaches to the Liberation of France* (London, Tiger Books International, 1993), p. 101; Derek Blizard, *The Normandy Landings: D-Day The Invasion of Europe 6 June 1944* (London, Reed International Books, 1993), pp. 46-9.

6   Captain Harry C. Butcher, *Three Years with Eisenhower: The Personal Diary of Captain Harry C. Butcher, USNR, Naval Aide to General Eisenhower, 1942 to 1945* (London, Heinemann, 1946), p. 451.

7, 8, 9   WSRO, MP 3730.

10   Keith and Janet Smith, *Witterings Then and Now: East Wittering, Bracklesham and Earnley* (East Wittering, Mill Press, 1985), pp. 74-5.

11   See source 9 for Chapter 2.

12   WRSO, MP 3730.

SOURCES

13 Joan Strange, *Despatches from the Home Front :
    The War Diaries of Joan Strange 1939-1945*
    [Worthing] (Eastbourne, Monarch
    Publications, 1989), pp. 142-3.

14 WSRO, Add. Ms. 46, 432, p. 159.

15 Strange, p. 143.

16 Alexander McKee, *Caen: Anvil of Victory*
    (London, White Lion, 1976), p. 24.

17 WSRO, Add. Ms. 1317; POL W/HQ15/5.

Chapter 4

1   PRO, WO 171/623.

2   Major-General Charles H. Miller, *History of the
    13th/18th Royal Hussars (Queen Mary's Own)
    1922-1947* (London, Chisman, Bradshaw,
    1949), pp. 86-7.

3   Friedrich Ruge, *Rommel in Normandy* (London,
    Macdonald and Jane's, 1979), p. 161.

4   Eisenhower, p. 234.

5   Ian Dear, *Ten Commando*
    (London, Leo Cooper, 1987).

6   Ellison, pp. 6, 9.

7   Chester Wilmot, *The Struggle for Europe*
    (London, Collins, 1952), p. 218.

8, 9, 10   WSRO, MP 3730.

11 PRO, WO 171/1300; 171/1262.

Chapter 5

1   Robin J. Brooks, *Sussex Airfields in the Second
    World War* (Newbury, Countryside Books,
    1993), pp. 149, 164.

2   WSRO, Add. Ms. 46, 345; Chris Ashworth,
    *Action Stations 9: Military airfields of the Central
    South and South-East* (Wellingborough, Patrick
    Stephens, 1985), pp. 44-5; Brooks, pp. 149-

53; Ken Rimell, *Merlin & the Sabre:
    The Story of Royal Air Force Apuldram 1943-1945*
    (Apuldram, the author, 1992).

3   Ashworth, pp. 252-3; Brooks, pp. 163-4;
    Frances Mee, *A History of Selsey* (Chichester,
    Phillimore, 1988), p. 106.

4   Information from Barbara Bertram of
    Petworth and Barbara Brimblecombe of
    Bignor; Ashworth, pp. 269-70; Brooks, p. 62;
    Andy Saunders, *RAF Tangmere in old
    Photographs* (Stroud, Alan Sutton, 1992), p. 92.

5   Lieutenant-General Sir Frederick Morgan,
    Overture to Overlord (London, Hodder and
    Stoughton, 1950), p. 161.

6   PRO, Air 28/815.

7   Ashworth, pp. 68-70; Brooks, pp. 156-8.

8   Ashworth, pp. 119-21; Brooks, pp. 60-2.

9   PRO, Air 28/815.

10 Information from Pamela Waldy of Petworth.

11 Heather Warne and Trevor Brighton,
    *A Portrait of Bishop Otter College Chichester
    1839-1990* (Chichester, West Sussex Institute
    of Higher Education, 1992), pp. 75-81.

12 *Bishop Otter College Journal* (RAF Edition No. 2,
    September 1944), quoted in Warne and
    Brighton, p. 80.

Chapter 6

1   WSRO, POL W/HQ15/5.

2   WSRO, MP 3740; Mee, pp. 107-8.

3   *Daily Sketch,* 23 October 1944.

4   Gerald Pawle, *Secret War 1939-45*
    (London, Harrap, 1956), p. 254.

5   Winston S. Churchill, *The Second World War:*

SOURCES

Volume V: Closing the Ring (London, Cassell, 4th edition, 1983), p. 66; facsimile of the minute, facing p. 78.

6 WSRO, MP 3730.

7 Pawle, p. 272.

8 Rémy Desquesnes, *Arromanches and the artificial ports* (Bayeux, Heimdal, 1980).

9 WSRO, MP 3730.

10 Joan Ham, *Sullington: Domesday to D-Day* (Storrington, the author, 1992), pp. 33, 302.

11 WSRO, MP 3730.

12 Diana Cooper, *Trumpets from the Steep* (London, Rupert Hart-Davis, 1960), pp. 194-5.

13 *Bognor Regis Observer,* 21 October 1944.

14 Gerard Young, 'Things on the Beach' in *Bognor Regis Post,* 17 August 1963; *Bognor Regis Local History Society Newsletter,* Nos. 11, 12 (July 1984, March 1985). The most detailed published information on the Mulberry wrecks off Bognor and Pagham is in Kendall McDonald, *Dive Sussex: A Diver Guide* (London, Underwater World Publications, 1985), pp. 52-65. The problem of dealing with the temporary sinking of the Phoenix caissons, some of which were abandoned, is described by Nicholas Thornton in *Sussex Shipwrecks* (Newbury, Countryside Books, 1988), pp. 19-24.

15 Desquesnes.

16 Pawle, p. 287.

17 PRO, DEFE 2/425.

18 WSRO, MP 3730.

Chapter 7

1 Ruge, p.167.

2 WSRO, MP 3730.

3 *The Midhurst Magazine,* Volume 2, No. 1 (Autumn 1989), p. 20.

4 Eisenhower, p. 243.

5 Bernard Darwin, *War on the Line: The Story of the Southern Railway in War-Time* (London, Southern Railway Company, 1946), p. 121.

6 WSRO, MP 3730.

7 Bernard L. Montgomery, *The Memoirs of Field-Marshal The Viscount Montgomery of Alamein, KG* (London, Collins, 1958), p. 234.

8 Wilmot, p. 221.

9 Eisenhower, p. 244.

10 WSRO, MP 3730.

11 N. Mason, 2nd Battalion, The East Yorkshire Regiment, quoted in Philip Warner, *The D-Day Landings* (London, Kimber, 1980), p. 175.

12 WSRO, MP 3730.

13 Warner, p. 272.

14 Cornelius Ryan, *The Longest Day* (London, Victor Gollanz, 1960), p. 54.

15 W.G.F. Jackson, *'Overlord': Normandy 1944* (London, Davis-Poynter, 1978), p. 169; Ruge, pp. 169, 171.

16 Wilmot, p. 229.

17 Montgomery, p. 249.

18 Information from Pamela Waldy of Petworth.

SOURCES

Chapter 8

1, 2 WSRO, MP 3730.

3   Keith Andreeti, *Wartime Voices: Memories of the Home Front in Worthing* (Worthing, Worthing Museum, 1989), pp. 38-9.

4   WSRO, Add. Ms. 35, 417.

5   Alan Wood, *History of the World's Glider Forces* (Wellingborough, Patrick Stephens, 1990), pp. 75-6.

6   Andreeti, p. 39; Wood, p. 81.

7   WSRO, MP 3730.

8   Strange, p. 145.

9,10 WSRO, MP 3730.

11   Winston S. Churchill, *The Second World War: Volume VI: Triumph and Tragedy* (London, Cassell, 1954), pp. 5-6.

12   Miller, p. 97.

13   M.E. Mawson, 13/18th Royal Hussars, quoted in Warner, pp. 135-6.

14   Lieutenant David Holbrook, the East Riding Yeomanry, quoted in Warner, pp. 206-9.

15   Private Richard Harris, B Company, 1st Battalion, The Suffolk Regiment, quoted in Warner, p. 183.

16   Badsey, p. 166.

17   Warner, p. 24.

18   Badsey, p. 166.

19   Badsey, p. 132.

20, 21, 22 WSRO, MP 3730.

PHOTOGRAPH REFERENCES

Abbreviations used:

BOCA Bishop Otter College Archives, Chichester
IWM Imperial War Museum, London
NAC National Archives of Canada, Ottawa
WSRO West Sussex Record Office, Chichester

1 IWM H38318
2 IWM KX17917
3 IWM H38987
4 WSRO PH14178
5 IWM H38878
6 IWM H38873
7 IWM H2962
8 IWM EA34392
9 IWM AP15393
10 IWM H31039
11 IWM HU42200
12 IWM MH2012
13 WSRO PH14179
14 WSRO PH750
15 WSRO PH9352
16 IWM H37860
17 IWM H38079
18 IWM H38419
19 WSRO MP1253
20 WSRO PH14181
21 WSRO PH14182
22 WSRO PH14183
23 IWM EN23839
24 IWM H38256
25 NAC PA140214
26 NAC PA140215
27 IWM H38294
28 WSRO Add. Ms. 1928
29 WSRO PH216
30 WRSO PH14184
31 IWM H38758
32 IWM H38755
33 IWM H38756
34 IWM H38760
35 IWM CH12859
36 IWM CH18722
37 WSRO PH14185
38 WSRO Add. Ms. 46345
39 WSRO PH14186
40 WSRO PH14187

SOURCES

41 IWM CH12857

42 IWM CH12855

43 IWM CH12890

44 IWM CH12889

45 WSRO PH14188

46 BOCA PH R/410

47 BOCA PH R/409

48 IWM H39292

49 WSRO PH14190

50 WSRO PH14191

51 IWM A25827

52 IWM A25824

53 IWM A25831

54 IWM H39310

55 IWM H39302

56 WSRO PH14192

57 IWM B5718

58 IWM B6062

59 IWM C4663

60 IWM B7240

61 WSRO PH14198

62 IWM H38785

63 IWM H38780

64 IWM H38324

65 IWM H38965

66 IWM H38987

67 IWM H38988

68 WSRO PH14193

69 WSRO PH14194

70 IWM AP25500

71 IWM B5207

72 IWM AP25496

73 WSRO RSR Ms. 9/49

74 IWM NYT27247

75 IWM CL19

76 IWM MH2072

77 IWM PL25582

78 WSRO PH14195

79 IWM B5114

80 IWM B5103

81 IWM A23938

82 IWM MH3097

83 IWM B5091

84 WSRO PH14196

85 WSRO PH14197

86 WSRO RSR Ms. 9/50

87 WSRO RSR Ms. 9/50

The following have kindly made available
photographs for inclusion in this book which have
been copied and added to the photographic
collection of the West Sussex Record Office:

D. Robert Elleray (4, 69)

Ron Ham (21)

Ron Iden (56)

Tony Liskutin (37, 39. 40)

Mary Lochner (49, 50)

Phillimore and Co. Ltd., Chichester (20)

Popperfoto, London (45)

Flora MacDonald Roberts (84, 85)

Ship Hotel, Chichester (19)

Solo Syndication Group, London (78)

INDEX

INDEX

INDEX

INDEX

INDEX

INDEX

INDEX

INDEX

INDEX

INDEX

INDEX

INDEX